GOD'S ANSWERS

for Your Life

GOD'S ANSWERS

for Your Life

WORD PUBLISHING
Dallas • London • Vancouver • Melbourne

GOD'S ANSWERS FOR YOUR LIFE

Unless otherwise noted, Scripture quotations are from *The Holy Bible, King James Version.*

Compiled and edited by Kay Wheeler Kilgore.

Library of Congress Cataloging-in-Publication Data

God's answers for your life.
p. cm.
ISBN 0-8499-5131-3 (tradepaper)
ISBN 0-8499-5307-3 (S.E.)
1. Christian life—Biblical teaching. 2. Bible N.T.—Use.
248.4—dc20 95–11753
CIP

Printed in the United States of America

6789 OPM 98765

Contents

4. Ministering In Christ • 167

5. Hoping In Christ • 217

6. Understanding In Christ • 239

7. Uniting In Christ • 265

Beginning In Christ...

BEGINNING IN CHRIST

How To Know You Are Born-Again

That if thou shalt confess with thy mouth the Lord Jesus, and shalt believe in thine heart that God hath raised him from the dead, thou shalt be saved.

For with the heart man believeth unto righteousness; and with the mouth confession is made unto salvation.

For the scripture saith, Whosoever believeth on him shall not be ashamed.

Romans 10:9-11

Verily, verily, I say unto you, He that heareth my word, and believeth on him that sent me, hath everlasting life, and shall not come into condemnation; but is passed from death unto life.

John 5:24

Therefore if any man be in Christ, he is a new creature: old things are passed away; behold, all things are become new.

II Corinthians 5:17

For by grace are ye saved through faith; and that not of yourselves: it is the gift of God:

Not of works, lest any man should boast.

For we are his workmanship, created in Christ Jesus unto good works, which God hath before ordained that we should walk in them.

Ephesians 2:8-10

Whosoever believeth that Jesus is the Christ is born of God: and every one that loveth him that begat loveth him also that is begotten of him.

By this we know that we love the children of God, when we love God, and keep his commandments.

For this is the love of God, that we keep his commandments: and his commandments are not grievous.

For whatsoever is born of God overcometh the world: and this is the victory that overcometh the world, even our faith.

Who is he that overcometh the world, but he that believeth that Jesus is the Son of God?

This is he that came by water and blood, even Jesus Christ; not by water only, but by water and blood. And it is the Spirit that beareth witness, because the Spirit is truth.

He that hath the Son hath life; and he that hath not the Son of God hath not life.

I John 5:1-6, 12

Whosoever therefore shall confess me before men, him will I confess also before my Father which is in heaven.

And he that taketh not his cross, and followeth after me is not worthy of me.

He that findeth his life shall lose it: and he that loseth his life for my sake shall find it.

Matthew 10:32, 38-39

I am crucified with Christ: nevertheless I live; yet not I, but Christ liveth in me: and the life which I now live in the flesh I live by the faith of the Son of God, who loved me, and gave himself for me.

Galatians 2:20

Being born again, not of corruptible seed, but of incorruptible, by the word of God, which liveth and abideth for ever.

I Peter 1:23

For ye are all the children of God by faith in Christ Jesus.

For as many of you as have been baptized into Christ have put on Christ.

There is neither Jew nor Greek, there is neither bond nor free, there is neither male nor female: for ye are all one in Christ Jesus.

Galatians 3:26-28

And they that are Christ's have crucified the flesh with the affections and lusts.

If we live in the Spirit, let us also walk in the Spirit.

Galatians 5:24-25

A new heart also will I give you, and a new spirit will I put within you: and I will take away the stony heart out of your flesh, and I will give you an heart of flesh.

And I will put my spirit within you, and cause you to walk in my statutes, and ye shall keep my judgments, and do them.

Ezekiel 36:26-27

We know that we have passed from death unto life, because we love the brethren. He that loveth not his brother abideth in death.

I John 3:14

But he that received seed into the good ground is he that heareth the word, and understandeth it; which also beareth fruit, and bringeth forth, some an hundred-fold, some sixty, some thirty.

Matthew 13:23

Knowing this, that our old man is crucified with him, that the body of sin might be destroyed, that henceforth we should not serve sin.

For he that is dead is freed from sin.

Now if we be dead with Christ, we believe that we shall also live with him:

Romans 6:6-8

And that ye put on the new man, which after God is created in righteousness and true holiness.

Ephesians 4:24

Fight the good fight of faith, lay hold on eternal life, whereunto thou art also called, and hast professed a good profession before many witnesses.

I Timothy 6:12

Let us hold fast the profession of our faith without wavering; (for he is faithful that promised;)

Hebrews 10:23

If ye know that he is righteous, ye know that every one that doeth righteousness is born of him.

I John 2:29

He that loveth not knoweth not God: for God is love.

I John 4:8

But as many as received him, to them gave he power to become the sons of God, even to them that believe on his name:

John 1:12

Jesus answered and said unto him, Verily, verily, I say unto thee, Except a man be born again, he cannot see the kingdom of God.

John 3:3

How To Know The Sufficiency of Jesus

Looking unto Jesus the author and finisher of our faith; who for the joy that was set before him endured the cross, despising the shame, and is set down at the right hand of the throne of God.

Hebrews 12:2

And Jesus said unto them, I am the bread of life: he that cometh to me shall never hunger; and he that believeth on me shall never thirst.

John 6:35

Let your conversation be without covetousness; and be content with such things as ye have: for he hath said, I will never leave thee, nor forsake thee.

So that we may boldly say, The Lord is my helper, and I will not fear what man shall do unto me.

Jesus Christ the same yesterday, and today, and for ever.

Hebrews 13:5-6, 8

Seeing then that we have a great high priest, that is passed into the heavens, Jesus the Son of God, let us hold fast our profession.

For we have not an high priest which cannot be touched with the feeling of our infirmities; but was in all points tempted like as we are, yet without sin.

Let us therefore come boldly unto the throne of grace, that we may obtain mercy, and find grace to help in time of need.

Hebrews 4:14-16

And he said unto me, My grace is sufficient for thee: for my strength is made perfect in weakness. Most gladly therefore will I rather glory in my infirmities, that the power of Christ may rest upon me.

II Corinthians 12:9

And Jesus came and spake unto them, saying, All power is given unto me in heaven and in earth.

Go ye therefore, and teach all nations, baptizing them in the name of the Father, and of the Son, and of the Holy Ghost:

Teaching them to observe all things whatsoever I have commanded you: and, lo, I am with you alway, even unto the end of the world. Amen.

Matthew 28:18-20

. . .Fear not; I am the first and the last:

I am he that liveth, and was dead; and, behold, I am alive for evermore, Amen; and have the keys of hell and of death.

Revelation 1:17-18

I can do all things through Christ which strengtheneth me.

Philippians 4:13

For in him dwelleth all the fulness of the Godhead bodily.

And ye are complete in him, which is the head of all principality and power:

Colossians 2:9-10

I am the good shepherd: the good shepherd giveth his life for the sheep.

John 10:11

THE LORD is my shepherd; I shall not want.

He maketh me to lie down in green pastures: he leadeth me beside the still waters.

He restoreth my soul: he leadeth me in the paths of righteousness for his name's sake.

Yea, though I walk through the valley of the shadow of death, I will fear no evil: for thou art with me; thy rod and thy staff they comfort me.

Psalm 23:1-4

If the Son therefore shall make you free, ye shall be free indeed.

John 8:36

And such trust have we through Christ to God-ward:

Not that we are sufficient of ourselves to think any thing as of ourselves; but our sufficiency is of God;

II Corinthians 3:4-5

... The Lord stood with me, and strengthened me; that by me the preaching might be fully known, and that all the Gentiles might hear: and I was delivered out of the mouth of the lion.

And the Lord shall deliver me from every evil work, and will preserve me unto his heavenly kingdom: to whom be glory for ever and ever. Amen.

II Timothy 4:17-18

My help cometh from the LORD, which made heaven and earth.

He will not suffer thy foot to be moved: he that keepeth thee will not slumber.

Psalm 121:2-3

Jesus saith unto him, I am the way, the truth, and the life: no man cometh unto the Father, but by me.

John 14:6

In him was life; and the life was the light of men.

John 1:4

According to the grace of God which is given unto me, as a wise masterbuilder, I have laid the foundation, and another buildeth thereon. But let every man take heed how he buildeth thereupon.

For other foundation can no man lay than that is laid, which is Jesus Christ.

I Corinthians 3:10-11

The night is far spent, the day is at hand: let us therefore cast off the works of darkness, and let us put on the armour of light.

Let us walk honestly, as in the day; not in rioting and drunkenness, not in chambering and wantonness, not in strife and envying.

But put ye on the Lord Jesus Christ, and make not provision for the flesh, to fulfil the lusts thereof.

Romans 13:12-14

The LORD is thy keeper: the LORD is thy shade upon thy right hand.

The LORD shall preserve thee from all evil: he shall preserve thy soul.

The LORD shall preserve thy going out and thy coming in from this time forth, and even for evermore.

Psalm 121:5, 7-8

Therefore doth my Father love me, because I lay down my life, that I might take it again.

No man taketh it from me, but I lay it down of myself. I have power to lay it down, and I have power to take it again. This commandment have I received of my Father.

John 10:17-18

The next day John seeth Jesus coming unto him, and saith, Behold the Lamb of God, which taketh away the sin of the world.

This is he of whom I said, After me cometh a man which is preferred before me: for he was before me.

John 1:29-30

Whom have I in heaven but thee? and there is none upon earth that I desire beside thee.

My flesh and my heart faileth: but God is the strength of my heart, and my portion for ever.

Psalm 73:25-26

For there is one God, and one mediator between God and men, the man Christ Jesus.

1 Timothy 2:5

What The Blood Of Jesus Is To You

For this is my blood of the new testament, which is shed for many for the remission of sins.

Matthew 26:28

Being justified freely by his grace through the redemption that is in Christ Jesus:

Whom God hath set forth to be a propitiation through faith in his blood, to declare his righteousness for the remission of sins that are past, through the forbearance of God;

To declare, I say, at this time his righteousness: that he might be just, and the justifier of him which believeth in Jesus.

Romans 3:24-26

For the life of the flesh is in the blood: and I have given it to you upon the altar to make an atonement for your souls: for it is the blood that maketh an atonement for the soul.

Leviticus 17:11

But God commendeth his love toward us, in that, while we were yet sinners, Christ died for us.

Much more then, being now justified by his blood, we shall be saved from wrath through him.

For if, when we were enemies, we were reconciled to God by the death of his Son, much more, being reconciled, we shall be saved by his life.

Romans 5:8-10

But if we walk in the light, as he is in the light, we have fellowship one with another, and the blood of Jesus Christ his Son cleanseth us from all sin.

I John 1:7

How much more shall the blood of Christ, who through the eternal Spirit offered himself without spot to God, purge your conscience from dead works to serve the living God?

Hebrews 9:14

Then Jesus said unto them, Verily, verily, I say unto you, Except ye eat the flesh of the Son of man, and drink his blood, ye have no life in you.

Whoso eateth my flesh, and drinketh my blood, hath eternal life; and I will raise him up at the last day.

He that eateth my flesh, and drinketh my blood, dwelleth in me, and I in him.

John 6:53, 54, 56

In whom we have redemption through his blood, the forgiveness of sins, according to the riches of his grace:

Ephesians 1:7

Moreover he sprinkled with blood both the tabernacle, and all the vessels of the ministry.

And almost all things are by the law purged with blood; and without shedding of blood is no remission.

Hebrews 9:21-22

Forasmuch as ye know that ye were not redeemed with corruptible things, as silver and gold, from your vain conversation received by tradition from your fathers;

But with the precious blood of Christ, as of a lamb without blemish and without spot:

Who verily was foreordained before the foundation of the world, but was manifest in these last times for you,

Who by him do believe in God, that raised him up from the dead, and gave him glory; that your faith and hope might be in God.

I Peter 1:18-21

And the blood shall be to you for a token upon the houses where ye are: and when I see the blood, I will pass over you, and the plague shall not be upon you to destroy you, when I smite the land of Egypt.

Exodus 12:13

And Moses took the blood, and sprinkled it on the people, and said, Behold the blood of the covenant which the LORD hath made with you concerning all these words.

Exodus 24:8

And he took bread, and gave thanks, and brake it, and gave unto them, saying, This is my body which is given for you: this do in remembrance of me.

Likewise also the cup after supper, saying, This cup is the new testament in my blood, which is shed for you.

Luke 22:19-20

But now in Christ Jesus ye who sometimes were far off are made nigh by the blood of Christ.

Ephesians 2:13

How To Know The Power Of The Word

For the word of God is quick, and powerful, and sharper than any two-edged sword, piercing even to the dividing asunder of soul and spirit, and of the joints and marrow, and is a discerner of the thoughts and intents of the heart.

Hebrews 4:12

Thy word have I hid in mine heart, that I might not sin against thee.

I will delight myself in thy statutes: I will not forget thy word.

Psalm 119:11, 16

How sweet are thy words unto my taste! yea, sweeter than honey to my mouth!

Through thy precepts I get understanding: therefore I hate every false way.

Thy word is a lamp unto my feet, and a light unto my path.

Psalm 119:103-105

The words of the LORD are pure words: as silver tried in a furnace of earth, purified seven times.

Thou shalt keep them, O LORD, thou shalt preserve them from this generation for ever.

Psalm 12:6-7

In the beginning was the Word, and the Word was with God, and the Word was God.

The same was in the beginning with God.

All things were made by him; and without him was not any thing made that was made.

In him was life; and the life was the light of men.

John 1:1-4

And that from a child thou hast known the holy scriptures, which are able to make thee wise unto salvation through faith which is in Christ Jesus.

All scripture is given by inspiration of God, and is profitable for doctrine, for reproof, for correction, for instruction in righteousness:

That the man of God may be perfect, thoroughly furnished unto all good works.

II Timothy 3:15-17

By the word of the LORD were the heavens made; and all the host of them by the breath of his mouth.

Psalm 33:6

He sent his word, and healed them, and delivered them from their destructions.

Oh that men would praise the LORD for his goodness, and for his wonderful works to the children of men!

Psalm 107:20-21

For ever, O LORD, thy word is settled in heaven.

Thy faithfulnes is unto all generations: thou hast established the earth, and it abideth.

Psalm 119:89-90

Thy testimonies are wonderful: therefore doth my soul keep them.

The entrance of thy words giveth light; it giveth understanding unto the simple.

Psalm 119:129-130

As newborn babes, desire the sincere milk of the word, that ye may grow thereby:

If so be ye have tasted that the Lord is gracious.

I Peter 2:2-3

Now ye are clean through the word which I have spoken unto you.

John 15:3

Being born again, not of corruptible seed, but of incorruptible, by the word of God, which liveth and abideth for ever.

For all flesh is as grass, and all the glory of man as the flower of grass. The grass withereth, and the flower thereof falleth away:

But the word of the Lord endureth for ever. And this is the word which by the gospel is preached unto you.

I Peter 1:23-25

But he answered and said, It is written, Man shall not live by bread alone, but by every word that proceedeth out of the mouth of God.

Matthew 4:4

Heaven and earth shall pass away: but my words shall not pass away.

Luke 21:33

It is the spirit that quickeneth; the flesh profiteth nothing: the words that I speak unto you, they are spirit, and they are life.

John 6:63

Then said Jesus to those Jews which believed on him, If ye continue in my word, then are ye my disciples indeed;

And ye shall know the truth, and the truth shall make you free.

John 8:31-32

Through faith we understand that the worlds were framed by the word of God, so that things which are seen were not made of things which do appear.

Hebrews 11:3

The grass withereth, the flower fadeth: but the word of our God shall stand for ever.

Isaiah 40:8

Heaviness in the heart of man maketh it stoop: but a good word maketh it glad.

Proverbs 12:25

Sanctify them through thy truth: thy word is truth.

John 17:17

Hold fast the form of sound words, which thou hast heard of me, in faith and love which is in Christ Jesus.

II Timothy 1:13

So then faith cometh by hearing, and hearing by the word of God.

Romans 10:17

And be not conformed to this world: but be ye transformed by the renewing of your mind, that ye may prove what is that good, and acceptable, and perfect, will of God.

Romans 12:2

And your feet shod with the preparation of the gospel of peace;

Above all, taking the shield of faith, wherewith ye shall be able to quench all the fiery darts of the wicked.

And take the helmet of salvation, and the sword of the Spirit, which is the word of God:

Ephesians 6:15-17

What The Holy Spirit Is To You

But the fruit of the Spirit is love, joy, peace, long-suffering, gentleness, goodness, faith,

Meekness, temperance: against such there is no law.

And they that are Christ's have crucified the flesh with the affections and lusts.

If we live in the Spirit, let us also walk in the Spirit.

Galatians 5:22-25

But as it is written, Eye hath not seen, nor ear heard, neither have entered into the heart of man, the things which God hath prepared for them that love him.

But God hath revealed them unto us by his Spirit: for the Spirit searcheth all things, yea, the deep things of God.

For what man, knoweth the things of a man, save the spirit of man which is in him? even so the things of God knoweth no man, but the Spirit of God.

Now we have received, not the spirit of the world, but the spirit which is of God; that we might know the things that are freely given to us of God.

Which things also we speak, not in the words which man's wisdom teacheth, but which the Holy Ghost teacheth; comparing spiritual things with spiritual.

But the natural man receiveth not the things of the Spirit of God: for they are foolishness unto him: neither can he know them, because they are spiritually discerned.

I Corinthians 2:9-14

If ye shall ask any thing in my name, I will do it.

If ye love me, keep my commandments.

And I will pray the Father, and he shall give you another Comforter, that he may abide with you for ever;

Even the Spirit of truth; whom the world cannot receive, because it seeth him not, neither knoweth him: but ye know him; for he dwelleth with you, and shall be in you.

I will not leave you comfortless: I will come to you.

But the Comforter, which is the Holy Ghost, whom the Father will send in my name, he shall teach you all things, and bring all things to your remembrance, whatsoever I have said unto you.

John 14:14-18, 26

But if the Spirit of him that raised up Jesus from the dead dwell in you, he that raised up Christ from the dead shall also quicken your mortal bodies by his Spirit that dwelleth in you.

The Spirit itself beareth witness with our spirit, that we are the children of God:

And if children, then heirs; heirs of God, and joint-heirs with Christ; if so be that we suffer with him, that we may be also glorified together.

For I reckon that the sufferings of this present time are not worthy to be compared with the glory which shall be revealed in us.

Likewise the Spirit also helpeth our infirmities: for we know not what we should pray for as we ought: but the Spirit itself maketh intercession for us with groanings which cannot be uttered.

And he that searcheth the hearts knoweth what is the mind of the Spirit, because he maketh intercession for the saints according to the will of God.

Romans 8:11, 16-18, 26-27

And it shall come to pass in the last days, saith God, I will pour out of my Spirit upon all flesh: and your sons and your daughters shall prophesy, and your young men shall see visions, and your old men shall dream dreams:

And on my servants and on my handmaidens I will pour out in those days of my Spirit; and they shall prophesy:

Acts 2:17-18

Nevertheless I tell you the truth; It is expedient for you that I go away: for if I go not away, the Comforter will not come unto you; but if I depart, I will send him unto you.

And when he is come, he will reprove the world of sin, and of righteousness, and of judgment:

Of sin, because they believe not on me;

Of righteousness, because I go to my Father, and ye see me no more;

Of judgment, because the prince of this world is judged.

I have yet many things to say unto you, but ye cannot bear them now.

Howbeit when he, the Spirit of truth, is come, he will guide you into all truth: for he shall not speak of himself; but whatsoever he shall hear, that shall he speak: and he will shew you things to come.

He shall glorify me: for he shall receive of mine, and shall shew it unto you.

All things that the Father hath are mine: therefore said I, that he shall take of mine, and shall shew it unto you.

A little while, and ye shall not see me: and again, a little while, and ye shall see me, because I go to the Father.

John 16:7-16

For our gospel came not unto you in word only, but also in power, and in the Holy Ghost, and in much assurance; as ye know what manner of men we were among you for your sake.

And ye became followers of us, and of the Lord, having received the word in much affliction, with joy of the Holy Ghost:

I Thessalonians 1:5-6

For every one that asketh receiveth; and he that seeketh findeth; and to him that knocketh it shall be opened.

If a son shall ask bread of any of you that is a father, will he give him a stone? or if he ask a fish, will he for a fish give him a serpent?

Or if he shall ask an egg, will he offer him a scorpion?

If ye then, being evil, know how to give good gifts unto your children: how much more shall your heavenly Father give the Holy Spirit to them that ask him?

Luke 11:10-13

And being assembled together with them, commanded them that they should not depart from Jerusalem, but wait for the promise of the Father, which, saith he, ye have heard of me.

For John truly baptized with water; but ye shall be baptized with the Holy Ghost not many days hence.

When they therefore were come together they asked of him, saying Lord, wilt thou at this time restore again the kingdom to Israel?

And he said unto them, It is not for you to know the times or the seasons, which the Father hath put in his own power.

But ye shall receive power, after that the Holy Ghost is come upon you: and ye shall be witnesses unto me both in Jerusalem, and in all Judaea, and in Samaria, and unto the uttermost part of the earth.

Acts 1:4-8

For it is not ye that speak, but the Spirit of your Father which speaketh in you.

Matthew 10:20

So shall they fear the name of the LORD from the west, and his glory from the rising of the sun. When the enemy shall come in like a flood, the spirit of the LORD shall lift up a standard against him.

Isaiah 59:19

See that ye refuse not him that speaketh. For if they escaped not who refused him that spake on earth, much more shall not we escape, if we turn away from him that speaketh from heaven:

Hebrews 12:25

Who also hath made us able ministers of the new testament; not of the letter, but of the spirit: for the letter killeth, but the spirit giveth life.

Now the Lord is that Spirit: and where the Spirit of the Lord is, there is liberty.

But we all, with open face beholding as in a glass the glory of the Lord, are changed into the same image from glory to glory, even as by the Spirit of the Lord.

II Corinthians 3:6, 17-18

For the Holy Ghost shall teach you in the same hour what ye ought to say.

Luke 12:12

And when they had prayed, the place was shaken where they were assembled together; and they were all filled with the Holy Ghost, and they spake the word of God with boldness.

And the multitude of them that believed were of one heart and of one soul: neither said any of them that aught of the things which he possessed was his own; but they had all things common.

And with great power gave the apostles witness of the resurrection of the Lord Jesus: and great grace was upon them all.

Acts 4:31-33

Wherefore be ye not unwise, but understanding what the will of the Lord is.

And be not drunk with wine, wherein is excess; but be filled with the Spirit;

Speaking to yourselves in psalms and hymns and spiritual songs, singing and making melody in your heart to the Lord;

Giving thanks always for all things unto God and the Father in the name of our Lord Jesus Christ;

Ephesians 5:17-20

From whom the whole body fitly joined together and compacted by that which every joint supplieth, according to the effectual working in the measure of every part, maketh increase of the body unto the edifying of itself in love.

And grieve not the holy Spirit of God, whereby ye are sealed unto the day of redemption.

Ephesians 4:16, 30

Knowing this first, that no prophecy of the scripture is of any private interpretation.

For the prophecy came not in old time by the will of man: but holy men of God spake as they were moved by the Holy Ghost.

II Peter 1:20-21

But ye, beloved, building up yourselves on your most holy faith, praying in the Holy Ghost,

Keep yourselves in the love of God, looking for the mercy of our Lord Jesus Christ unto eternal life.

Jude 20, 21

And, behold, I send the promise of my Father upon you: but tarry ye in the city of Jerusalem, until ye be endued with power from on high.

Luke 24:49

How To Abide In Christ

Abide in me, and I in you. As the branch cannot bear fruit of itself, except it abide in the vine; no more can ye, except ye abide in me.

I am the vine, ye are the branches: He that abideth in me, and I in him, the same bringeth forth much fruit: for without me ye can do nothing.

If a man abide not in me, he is cast forth as a branch, and is withered; and men gather them and cast them into the fire, and they are burned.

If ye abide in me, and my words abide in you, ye shall ask what ye will, and it shall be done unto you.

John 15:4-7

And now, little children, abide in him; that, when he shall appear, we may have confidence, and not be ashamed before him at his coming.

I John 2:28

I love them that love me; and those that seek me early shall find me.

Proverbs 8:17

I will meditate in thy precepts, and have respect unto thy ways.

I will delight myself in thy statutes: I will not forget thy word.

Psalm 119:15-16

Let the word of Christ dwell in you richly in all wisdom; teaching and admonishing one another in psalms and hymns and spiritual songs, singing with grace in your hearts to the Lord.

Colossians 3:16

But they that wait upon the LORD shall renew their strength; they shall mount up with wings as eagles; they shall run, and not be weary; and they shall walk, and not faint.

Isaiah 40:31

And hereby we do know that we know him, if we keep his commandments.

He that saith, I know him, and keepeth not his commandments, is a liar, and the truth is not in him.

But whoso keepeth his word, in him verily is the love of God perfected: hereby know we that we are in him.

He that saith he abideth in him ought himself also so to walk, even as he walked.

I John 2:3-6

Draw nigh to God, and he will draw nigh to you. Cleanse your hands, ye sinners; and purify your hearts, ye double-minded.

James 4:8

For in him we live, and move, and have our being; as certain also of your own poets have said, For we are also his offspring.

Acts 17:28

Blessed is the man that heareth me, watching daily at my gates, waiting at the posts of my doors.

Proverbs 8:34

Till I come, give attendance to reading, to exhortation, to doctrine.

I Timothy 4:13

But put ye on the Lord Jesus Christ, and make not provision for the flesh, to fulfil the lusts thereof.

Romans 13:14

As newborn babes, desire the sincere milk of the word, that ye may grow thereby:

I Peter 2:2

But be ye doers of the word, and not hearers only, deceiving your own selves.

James 1:22

Speaking to yourselves in psalms and hymns and spiritual songs, singing and making melody in your heart to the Lord;

Giving thanks always for all things unto God and the Father in the name of our Lord Jesus Christ;

Ephesians 5:19-20

And ye know that he was manifested to take away our sins; and in him is no sin.

Whosoever abideth in him sinneth not: whosoever sinneth hath not seen him, neither known him.

I John 3:5-6

Whosoever transgresseth, and abideth not in the doctrine of Christ, hath not God. He that abideth in the doctrine of Christ, he hath both the Father and the Son.

II John 1:9

For all things are for your sakes, that the abundant grace might through the thanksgiving of many redound to the glory of God.

For which cause we faint not; but though our outward man perish, yet the inward man is renewed day by day.

II Corinthians 4:15-16

THEREFORE we ought to give the more earnest heed to the things which we have heard, lest at any time we should let them slip.

For if the word spoken by angels was stedfast, and every transgression and disobedience received a just recompence of reward;

How shall we escape, if we neglect so great salvation; which at the first began to be spoken by the Lord, and was confirmed unto us by them that heard him;

Hebrews 2:1-3

Looking unto Jesus the author and finisher of our faith; who for the joy that was set before him endured the cross, despising the shame, and is set down at the right hand of the throne of God.

Hebrews 12:2

How To Build Your Faith

Now faith is the substance of things hoped for, the evidence of things not seen.

Through faith we understand that the worlds were framed by the word of God, so that things which are seen were not made of things which do appear.

But without faith it is impossible to please him; for he that cometh to God must believe that he is, and that he is a rewarder of them that diligently seek him.

By faith he forsook Egypt, not fearing the wrath of the king: for he endured, as seeing him who is invisible.

Hebrews 11:1,3,6,27

That the trial of your faith, being much more precious than of gold that perisheth, though it be tried with fire, might be found unto praise and honour and glory at the appearing of Jesus Christ:

Whom having not seen, ye love; in whom, though now ye see him not, yet believing, ye rejoice with joy unspeakable and full of glory:

Receiving the end of your faith, even the salvation of your souls.

I Peter 1:7-9

For therein is the righteousness of God revealed from faith to faith: as it is written, The just shall live by faith.

Romans 1:17

Have not I commanded thee? Be strong and of a good courage; be not afraid, neither be thou dismayed: for the LORD thy God is with thee whithersoever thou goest.

Joshua 1:9

So then faith cometh by hearing, and hearing by the word of God.

Romans 10:17

If any of you lack wisdom, let him ask of God, that giveth to all men liberally, and upbraideth not; and it shall be given him.

But let him ask in faith, nothing wavering. For he that wavereth is like a wave of the sea driven with the wind and tossed.

For let not that man think that he shall receive any thing of the Lord.

A double-minded man is unstable in all his ways.

James 1:5-8

For with God nothing shall be impossible.

Luke 1:37

He staggered not at the promise of God through unbelief; but was strong in faith, giving glory to God;

And being fully persuaded that, what he had promised, he was able also to perform.

Romans 4:20-21

We are troubled on every side, yet not distressed; we are perplexed, but not in despair;

Persecuted, but not forsaken; cast down, but not destroyed;

Always bearing about in the body the dying of the Lord Jesus, that the life also of Jesus might be made manifest in our body.

II Corinthians 4:8-10

What shall we then say to these things? If God be for us, who can be against us?

Romans 8:31

But ye, beloved, building up yourselves on your most holy faith, praying in the Holy Ghost,

Keep yourselves in the love of God, looking for the mercy of our Lord Jesus Christ unto eternal life.

Jude 20,21

(For we walk by faith, not by sight:)

II Corinthians 5:7

Jesus said unto him, If thou canst believe, all things are possible to him that believeth.

Mark 9:23

Whom have I in heaven but thee? and there is none upon earth that I desire beside thee.

My flesh and my heart faileth: but God is the strength of my heart, and my portion for ever.

Psalm 73:25,26

Behold, I am the LORD, the God of all flesh: is there any thing too hard for me?

Jeremiah 32:27

Rejoice not against me, O mine enemy: when I fall, I shall arise; when I sit in darkness, the LORD shall be a light unto me.

Micah 7:8

Behold, his soul which is lifted up is not upright in him: but the just shall live by his faith.

Habakkuk 2:4

Yea, a man may say, Thou hast faith, and I have works: shew me thy faith without thy works, and I will shew thee my faith by my works.

Seest thou how faith wrought with his works, and by works was faith made perfect?

James 2:18, 22

Beloved, when I gave all diligence to write unto you of the common salvation, it was needful for me to write unto you, and exhort you that ye should earnestly contend for the faith which was once delivered unto the saints.

Jude 3

But call to remembrance the former days, in which, after ye were illuminated, ye endured a great fight of afflictions;

Cast not away therefore your confidence, which hath great recompence of reward.

For ye have need of patience, that, after ye have done the will of God, ye might receive the promise.

For yet a little while, and he that shall come will come, and will not tarry.

Now the just shall live by faith: but if any man draw back, my soul shall have no pleasure in him.

But we are not of them who draw back unto perdition; but of them that believe to the saving of the soul.

Hebrews 10:32,35-39

Growing In Christ . . .

How To Overcome The Carnal Mind

For the law of the Spirit of life in Christ Jesus hath made me free from the law of sin and death.

For what the law could not do, in that it was weak through the flesh, God sending his own Son in the likeness of sinful flesh, and for sin, condemned sin in the flesh:

That the righteousness of the law might be fulfilled in us, who walk not after the flesh, but after the Spirit.

For they that are after the flesh do mind the things of the flesh; but they that are after the Spirit the things of the Spirit.

For to be carnally minded is death; but to be spiritually minded is life and peace.

Because the carnal mind is enmity against God: for it is not subject to the law of God, neither indeed can be.

So then they that are in the flesh cannot please God.

But ye are not in the flesh, but in the Spirit, if so be that the Spirit of God dwell in you. Now if any man have not the Spirit of Christ, he is none of his.

And if Christ be in you, the body is dead because of sin; but the Spirit is life because of righteousness.

But if the Spirit of him that raised up Jesus from the dead dwell in you, he that raised up Christ from the dead shall also quicken your mortal bodies by his Spirit that dwelleth in you.

Therefore, brethren, we are debtors, not to the flesh, to live after the flesh.

For if ye live after the flesh, ye shall die: but if ye through the Spirit do mortify the deeds of the body, ye shall live.

Nay, in all these things we are more than conquerors through him that loved us.

Romans 8:2-13, 37

For, brethren, ye have been called unto liberty; only use not liberty for an occasion to the flesh, but by love serve one another.

For all the law is fulfilled in one word, even in this; Thou shalt love thy neighbour as thyself.

But if ye bite and devour one another, take heed that ye be not consumed one of another.

This I say then, Walk in the Spirit, and ye shall not fulfill the lust of the flesh.

For the flesh lusteth against the Spirit, and the Spirit against the flesh: and these are contrary the one to the other: so that ye cannot do the things that ye would.

Galatians 5:13-17

I BESEECH you therefore, brethren, by the mercies of God, that ye present your bodies a living sacrifice, holy, acceptable unto God, which is your reasonable service.

And be not conformed to this world: but be ye transformed by the renewing of your mind, that ye may prove what is that good, and acceptable, and perfect, will of God.

Romans 12:1-2

Wherefore gird up the loins of your mind, be sober, and hope to the end for the grace that is to be brought unto you at the revelation of Jesus Christ;

As obedient children, not fashioning yourselves according to the former lusts in your ignorance:

But as he which hath called you is holy, so be ye holy in all manner of conversation;

I Peter 1:13-15

I am crucified with Christ: nevertheless I live; yet not I, but Christ liveth in me: and the life which I now live in the flesh I live by the faith of the Son of God, who loved me, and gave himself for me.

Galatians 2:20

Thou wilt keep him in perfect peace, whose mind is stayed on thee: because he trusteth in thee.

Isaiah 26:3

Knowing this, that our old man is crucified with him, that the body of sin might be destroyed, that henceforth we should not serve sin.

Now if we be dead with Christ, we believe that we shall also live with him:

Knowing that Christ being raised from the dead dieth no more; death hath no more dominion over him.

Likewise reckon ye also yourselves to be dead indeed unto sin, but alive unto God through Jesus Christ our Lord.

Romans 6:6, 8, 9, 11

That ye put off concerning the former conversation the old man, which is corrupt according to the deceitful lusts;

And be renewed in the spirit of your mind;

And that ye put on the new man, which after God is created in righteousness and true holiness.

Ephesians 4:22-24

Let this mind be in you, which was also in Christ Jesus:

Philippians 2:5

Let us walk honestly, as in the day; not in rioting and drunkenness, not in chambering and wantonness, not in strife and envying.

But put ye on the Lord Jesus Christ, and make not provision for the flesh, to fulfil the lusts thereof.

Romans 13:13-14

For which cause we faint not; but though our outward man perish, yet the inward man is renewed day by day.

II Corinthians 4:16

Beware lest any man spoil you through philosophy and vain deceit, after the tradition of men, after the rudiments of the world, and not after Christ.

Colossians 2:8

Wherefore if thy hand or thy foot offend thee, cut them off, and cast them from thee: it is better for thee to enter into life halt or maimed, rather than having two hands or two feet to be cast into everlasting fire.

And if thine eye offend thee, pluck it out, and cast if from thee: it is better for thee to enter into life with one eye, rather than having two eyes to be cast into hell fire.

Matthew 18:8-9

For who hath known the mind of the Lord, that he may instruct him? But we have the mind of Christ.

I Corinthians 2:16

For if there be first a willing mind, it is accepted according to that a man hath, and not according to that he hath not.

II Corinthians 8:12

He that hath no rule over his own spirit is like a city that is broken down, and without walls.

Proverbs 25:28

"...remember all the commandments of the LORD, and do them; and that ye seek not after your own heart and your own eyes, after which ye use to go a-whoring:

That ye may remember, and do all my commandments, and be holy unto your God.

Numbers 15:39-40

But what things were gain to me, those I counted loss for Christ.

Yea doubtless, and I count all things but loss for the excellency of the knowledge of Christ Jesus my Lord: for whom I have suffered the loss of all things, and do count them but dung, that I may win Christ.

Philippians 3:7-8

And they that are Christ's have crucified the flesh with the affections and lusts.

If we live in the Spirit, let us also walk in the Spirit.

Galatians 5:24-25

But I keep under my body, and bring it into subjection: lest that by any means, when I have preached to others, I myself should be a castaway.

I Corinthians 9:27

Ye cannot drink the cup of the Lord, and the cup of devils: ye cannot be partakers of the Lord's table, and of the table of devils.

I Corinthians 10:21

There is a way which seemeth right unto a man, but the end thereof are the ways of death.

Proverbs 14:12

Finally, brethren, whatsoever things are true, whatsoever things are honest, whatsoever things are just, whatsoever things are pure, whatsoever things are lovely, whatsoever things are of good report; if there be any virtue, and if there be any praise, think on these things.

Philippians 4:8

How To Overcome Satan

Finally, my brethren, be strong in the Lord, and in the power of his might.

Put on the whole armour of God, that ye may be able to stand against the wiles of the devil.

For we wrestle not against flesh and blood, but against principalities, against powers, against the rulers of the darkness of this world, against spiritual wickedness in high places.

Wherefore take unto you the whole armour of God, that ye may be able to withstand in the evil day, and having done all, to stand.

Stand therefore, having your loins girt about with truth, and having on the breastplate of righteousness;

And your feet shod with the preparation of the gospel of peace;

Above all, taking the shield of faith, wherewith ye shall be able to quench all the fiery darts of the wicked.

And take the helmet of salvation, and the sword of the Spirit, which is the word of God:

Ephesians 6:10-17

Submit yourselves therefore to God. Resist the devil, and he will flee from you.

Draw nigh to God, and he will draw nigh to you. Cleanse your hands, ye sinners; and purify your hearts, ye double-minded.

James 4:7-8

And he said unto them, I beheld Satan as lightning fall from heaven.

Behold, I give you power to tread on serpents and scorpions and over all the power of the enemy: and nothing shall by any means hurt you.

Luke 10:18-19

Be sober, be vigilant; because your adversary the devil, as a roaring lion, walketh about, seeking whom he may devour:

Whom resist stedfast in the faith, knowing that the same afflictions are accomplished in your brethren that are in the world.

But the God of all grace, who hath called us unto his eternal glory by Christ Jesus, after that ye have suffered a while, make you perfect, stablish, strengthen, settle you.

I Peter 5:8-10

The LORD shall preserve thee from all evil: he shall preserve thy soul.

The LORD shall preserve thy going out and thy coming in from this time forth, and even for evermore.

Psalm 121:7-8

Surely he shall deliver thee from the snare of the fowler, and from the noisome pestilence.

He shall cover thee with his feathers, and under his wings shalt thou trust: his truth shall be thy shield and buckler.

Thou shalt not be afraid for the terror by night; nor for the arrow that flieth by day;

Nor for the pestilence that walketh in darkness; nor for the destruction that wasteth at noonday.

A thousand shall fall at thy side, and ten thousand at thy right hand; but it shall not come nigh thee.

Psalm 91:3-7

He that committeth sin is of the devil; for the devil sinneth from the beginning. For this purpose the Son of God was manifested, that he might destroy the works of the devil.

I John 3:8

And the peace of God, which passeth all understanding, shall keep your hearts and minds through Christ Jesus.

Finally, brethren, whatsoever things are true, whatsoever things are honest, whatsoever things are just, whatsoever things are pure, whatsoever things are lovely, whatsoever things are of good report; if there be any virtue, and if there be any praise, think on these things.

Philippians 4:7-8

BELOVED, believe not every spirit, but try the spirits whether they are of God: because many false prophets are gone out into the world.

Hereby know ye the Spirit of God: Every spirit that confesseth that Jesus Christ is come in the flesh is of God:

And every spirit that confesseth not that Jesus Christ is come in the flesh is not of God: and this is that spirit of antichrist, whereof ye have heard that it should come; and even now already is it in the world.

Ye are of God, little children, and have overcome them: because greater is he that is in you, than he that is in the world.

I John 4:1-4

To whom ye forgive any thing, I forgive also: for if I forgave any thing, to whom I forgave it, for your sakes forgave I it in the person of Christ;

Lest Satan should get an advantage of us: for we are not ignorant of his devices.

II Corinthians 2:10-11

Be ye angry, and sin not: let not the sun go down upon your wrath:

Neither give place to the devil.

Ephesians 4:26-27

But the Lord is faithful, who shall stablish you, and keep you from evil.

II Thessalonians 3:3

And the Lord shall deliver me from every evil work, and will preserve me unto his heavenly kingdom: to whom be glory for ever and ever. Amen.

II Timothy 4:18

Nay, in all these things we are more than conquerors through him that loved us.

Romans 8:37

To him that overcometh will I grant to sit with me in my throne, even as I also overcame, and am set down with my Father in his throne.

Revelation 3:21

And the devil that deceived them was cast into the lake of fire and brimstone, where the beast and the false prophet are, and shall be tormented day and night for ever and ever.

Revelation 20:10

For in that he himself hath suffered being tempted, he is able to succour them that are tempted.

Hebrews 2:18

But seek ye first the kingdom of God, and his righteousness; and all these things shall be added unto you.

Take therefore no thought for the morrow: for the morrow shall take thought for the things of itself. Sufficient unto the day is the evil thereof.

Matthew 6:33-34

Beware of false prophets, which come to you in sheep's clothing, but inwardly they are ravening wolves.

Ye shall know them by their fruits. Do men gather grapes of thorns, or figs of thistles?

Even so every good tree bringeth forth good fruit; but a corrupt tree bringeth forth evil fruit.

Matthew 7:15-17

Behold, I send you forth as sheep in the midst of wolves: be ye therefore wise as serpents, and harmless as doves.

Matthew 10:16

Not a novice, lest being lifted up with pride he fall into the condemnation of the devil.

Moreover he must have a good report of them which are without; lest he fall into reproach and the snare of the devil.

I Timothy 3:6-7

How To Recognize Evil

Beware of false prophets, which come to you in sheep's clothing, but inwardly they are ravening wolves.

Ye shall know them by their fruits. Do men gather grapes of thorns, or figs of thistles?

Even so every good tree bringeth forth good fruit; but a corrupt tree bringeth forth evil fruit.

Wherefore by their fruits ye shall know them.

Not every one that saith unto me, Lord, Lord, shall enter into the kindgom of heaven; but he that doeth the will of my Father which is in heaven.

Many will say to me in that day, Lord, Lord, have we not prophesied in thy name? and in thy name have cast out devils? and in thy name done many wonderful works?

And then will I profess unto them, I never knew you: depart from me, ye that work iniquity.

Matthew 7:15-17, 20-23

BELOVED, believe not every spirit, but try the spirits whether they are of God: because many false prophets are gone out into the world.

Hereby know ye the Spirit of God: Every spirit that confesseth that Jesus Christ is come in the flesh is of God:

And every spirit that confesseth not that Jesus Christ is come in the flesh is not of God: and this is that spirit of antichrist, whereof ye have heard that it should come; and even now already is it in the world.

I John 4:1-3

And when they shall say unto you, Seek unto them that have familiar spirits, and unto wizards that peep, and that mutter: should not a people seek unto their God? for the living to the dead?

To the law and to the testimony: if they speak not according to this word, it is because there is no light in them.

Isaiah 8:19-20

Behold, I am against them that prophesy false dreams, saith the LORD, and do tell them, and cause my people to err by their lies, and by their lightness; yet I sent them not, nor commanded them: therefore they shall not profit this people at all, saith the LORD.

Jeremiah 23:32

For a good tree bringeth not forth corrupt fruit; neither doth a corrupt tree bring forth good fruit.

For every tree is known by his own fruit. For of thorns men do not gather figs, nor of a bramble bush gather they grapes.

Luke 6:43-44

For God is not the author of confusion, but of peace, as in all churches of the saints.

I Corinthians 14:33

For God hath not given us the spirit of fear; but of power, and of love and of a sound mind.

II Timothy 1:7

STAND fast therefore in the liberty wherewith Christ hath made us free, and be not entangled again with the yoke of bondage.

Galatians 5:1

He is a merchant, the balances of deceit are in his hand: he loveth to oppress.

Hosea 12:7

They profess that they know God; but in works they deny him, being abominable, and disobedient, and unto every good work reprobate.

Titus 1:16

He that committeth sin is of the devil; for the devil sinneth from the beginning. For this purpose the Son of God was manifested, that he might destroy the works of the devil.

In this the children of God are manifest, and the children of the devil: whosoever doeth not righteousness is not of God, neither he that loveth not his brother.

I John 3:8,10

For many deceivers are entered into the world, who confess not that Jesus Christ is come in the flesh. This is a deceiver and an an-ti-christ.

Whosoever transgresseth, and abideth not in the doctrine of Christ, hath not God. He that abideth in the doctrine of Christ, he hath both the Father and the Son.

If there come any unto you, and bring not this doctrine, receive him not into your house, neither bid him God speed:

For he that biddeth him God speed is partaker of his evil deeds.

II John 1:7, 9-11

Desiring to be teachers of the law; understanding neither what they say, nor whereof they affirm.

I Timothy 1:7

His heart is as firm as a stone; yea, as hard as a piece of the nether millstone.

He beholdeth all high things: he is a king over all the children of pride.

Job 41:24,34

Whom shall he teach knowledge? and whom shall he make to understand doctrine? them that are weaned from the milk, and drawn from the breasts.

Isaiah 28:9

And thou shalt take no gift: for the gift blindeth the wise, and perverteth the words of the righteous.

Exodus 23:8

For there are certain men crept in unawares, who were before of old ordained to this condemnation, ungodly men, turning the grace of our God into lasciviousness, and denying the only Lord God, and our Lord Jesus Christ.

Jude 4

How To Overcome Worldliness

No man can serve two masters: for either he will hate the one, and love the other; or else he will hold to the one, and despise the other. Ye cannot serve God and mam-mon.

Matthew 6:24

Love not the world, neither the things that are in the world. If any man love the world, the love of the Father is not in him.

For all that is in the world, the lust of the flesh, and the lust of the eyes, and the pride of life, is not of the Father, but is of the world.

And the world passeth away, and the lust thereof: but he that doeth the will of God abideth for ever.

I John 2:15-17

And be not conformed to this world: but be ye transformed by the renewing of your mind, that ye may prove what is that good, and acceptable, and perfect, will of God.

Romans 12:2

And that, knowing the time, that now it is high time to awake out of sleep: for now is our salvation nearer than when we believed.

The night is far spent, the day is at hand: let us therefore cast off the works of darkness, and let us put on the armour of light.

Let us walk honestly, as in the day; not in rioting and drunkenness, not in chambering and wantonness, not in strife and envying.

But put ye on the Lord Jesus Christ, and make not provision for the flesh, to fulfil the lusts thereof.

Romans 13:11-14

And have no fellowship with the unfruitful works of darkness, but rather reprove them.

Ephesians 5:11

The Lord knoweth how to deliver the godly out of temptations, and to reserve the unjust unto the day of judgment to be punished:

II Peter 2:9

And he said to them all, If any man will come after me, let him deny himself, and take up his cross daily, and follow me.

For whosoever will save his life shall lose it: but whosoever will lose his life for my sake, the same shall save it.

For what is a man advantaged, if he gain the whole world, and lose himself, or be cast away?

Luke 9:23-25

Now therefore fear the LORD, and serve him in sincerity and in truth: and put away the gods which your fathers served on the other side of the flood, and in Egypt; and serve ye the LORD.

Joshua 24:14

Choosing rather to suffer affliction with the people of God, than to enjoy the pleasures of sin for a season;

Esteeming the reproach of Christ greater riches than the treasures in Egypt: for he had respect unto the recompence of the reward.

By faith he forsook Egypt, not fearing the wrath of the king: for he endured, as seeing him who is invisible.

Hebrews 11:25-27

Whereby are given unto us exceeding great and precious promises: that by these ye might be partakers of the divine nature, having escaped the corruption that is in the world through lust.

II Peter 1:4

And take heed to yourselves, lest at any time your hearts be overcharged with surfeiting, and drunkenness, and cares of this life, and so that day come upon you unawares.

Luke 21:34

Set your affection on things above, not on things on the earth.

Lie not one to another, seeing that ye have put off the old man with his deeds;

And have put on the new man, which is renewed in knowledge after the image of him that created him:

Colossians 3:2, 9-10

There hath no temptation taken you but such as is common to man: but God is faithful, who will not suffer you to be tempted above that ye are able; but will with the temptation also make a way to escape, that ye may be able to bear it.

Ye cannot drink the cup of the Lord, and the cup of devils: ye cannot be partakers of the Lord's table, and of the table of devils.

I Corinthians 10:13, 21

But have renounced the hidden things of dishonesty, not walking in craftiness, nor handling the word of God deceitfully; but by manifestation of the truth commending ourselves to every man's conscience in the sight of God.

II Corinthians 4:2

Teaching us that, denying ungodliness and worldly lusts, we should live soberly, righteously, and godly, in this present world;

Looking for that blessed hope, and the glorious appearing of the great God and our Saviour Jesus Christ;

Titus 2:12-13

But what things were gain to me, those I counted loss for Christ.

Philippians 3:7

Who is he that overcometh the world, but he that believeth that Jesus is the Son of God?

I John 5:5

Wherefore, my beloved brethren, let every man be swift to hear, slow to speak, slow to wrath:

For the wrath of man worketh not the righteousness of God.

Wherefore lay apart all filthiness and superfluity of naughtiness, and receive with meekness the engrafted word, which is able to save your souls.

Pure religion and undefiled before God and the Father is this, To visit the fatherless and widows in their affliction, and to keep himself unspotted from the world.

James 1:19-21, 27

And he said unto them, Take heed, and beware of covetousness: for a man's life consisteh not in the abundance of the things which he possesseth.

Luke 12:15

Out of the same mouth proceedeth blessing and cursing. My brethren, these things ought not so to be.

Doth a fountain send forth at the same place sweet water and bitter?

James 3:10-11

Ye adulterers and adulteresses, know ye not that the friendship of the world is enmity with God? whosoever therefore will be a friend of the world is the enemy of God.

James 4:4

These things I have spoken unto you, that in me ye might have peace. In the world ye shall have tribulation: but be of good cheer; I have overcome the world.

John 16:33

Wine is a mocker, strong drink is raging: and whosoever is deceived thereby is not wise.

Proverbs 20:1

Hell and destruction are never full; so the eyes of man are never satisfied.

Proverbs 27:20

Woe to the rebellious children, saith the LORD, that take counsel, but not of me; and that cover with a covering, but not of my spirit, that they may add sin to sin:

Isaiah 30:1

Likewise reckon ye also yourselves to be dead indeed unto sin, but alive unto God through Jesus Christ our Lord.

Let not sin therefore reign in your mortal body, that ye should obey it in the lusts thereof.

Romans 6:11-12

Be ye not unequally yoked together with unbelievers: for what fellowship hath righteousness with unrighteousness? and what communion hath light with darkness?

And what concord hath Christ with Belial? or what part hath he that believeth with an infidel?

And what agreement hath the temple of God with idols? for ye are the temple of the living God; as God hath said, I will dwell in them, and walk in them; and I will be their God, and they shall be my people.

Wherefore come out from among them, and be ye separate, saith the Lord, and touch not the unclean thing; and I will receive you,

II Corinthians 6:14-17

And these are they which are sown among thorns; such as hear the word,

And the cares of this world, and the deceitfulness of riches, and the lusts of other things entering in, choke the word, and it becometh unfruitful.

And these are they which are sown on good ground; such as hear the word, and receive it, and bring forth fruit, some thirty-fold, some sixty, and some an hundred.

Mark 4:18-20

How To Deal With Lust

Know ye not that your bodies are the members of Christ? shall I then take the members of Christ, and make them the members of an harlot? God forbid.

What? know ye not that he which is joined to an harlot is one body? for two, saith he, shall be one flesh.

But he that is joined unto the Lord is one spirit.

Flee fornication. Every sin that a man doeth is without the body; but he that committeth fornication sinneth against his own body.

What? know ye not that your body is the temple of the Holy Ghost which is in you, which ye have of God, and ye are not your own?

For ye are bought with a price: therefore glorify God in your body, and in your spirit, which are God's.

I Corinthians 6:15-20

This I say then, Walk in the Spirit, and ye shall not fulfil the lust of the flesh.

For the flesh lusteth against the Spirit, and the Spirit against the flesh: and these are contrary the one to the other: so that ye cannot do the things that ye would.

Galatians 5:16-17

There hath no temptation taken you but such as is common to man: but God is faithful, who will not suffer you to be tempted above that ye are able; but will with the temptation also make a way to escape, that ye may be able to bear it.

I Corinthians 10:13

That ye put off concerning the former conversation the old man, which is corrupt according to the deceitful lusts;

And be renewed in the spirit of your mind;

And that ye put on the new man, which after God is created in righteousness and true holiness.

Neither give place to the devil.

Ephesians 4:22-24, 27

Submit yourselves therefore to God. Resist the devil, and he will flee from you.

James 4:7

But every man is tempted, when he is drawn away of his own lust, and enticed.

Then when lust hath conceived, it bringeth forth sin: and sin, when it is finished, bringeth forth death.

Do not err, my beloved brethren.

Every good gift and every perfect gift is from above, and cometh down from the Father of lights, with whom is no variableness, neither shadow of turning.

Lust not after her beauty in thine heart; neither let her take thee with her eyelids.

For by means of a whorish woman a man is brought to a piece of bread: and the adulteress will hunt for the precious life.

Proverbs 6:25-26

Hearken unto me now therefore, O ye children, and attend to the words of my mouth.

Let not thine heart decline to her ways, go not astray in her paths.

For she hath cast down many wounded: yea, many strong men have been slain by her.

Her house is the way to hell, going down to the chambers of death.

Proverbs 7:24-27

The Lord knoweth how to deliver the godly out of temptations, and to reserve the unjust unto the day of judgment to be punished:

II Peter 2:9

My brethren, count it all joy when ye fall into divers temptations;

Knowing this, that the trying of your faith worketh patience.

But let patience have her perfect work, that ye may be perfect and entire, wanting nothing.

James 1:2-4

For we have not an high priest which cannot be touched with the feeling of our infirmities; but was in all points tempted like as we are, yet without sin.

Hebrews 4:15

(For the weapons of our warfare are not carnal, but mighty through God to the pulling down of strong holds;)

II Corinthians 10:4

He that is greedy of gain troubleth his own house; but he that hateth gifts shall live.

The LORD is far from the wicked: but he heareth the prayer of the righteous.

Proverbs 15:27, 29

And they come to Jerusalem: and Jesus went into the temple, and began to cast out them that sold and bought in the temple, and overthrew the tables of the moneychangers, and the seats of them that sold doves;

And he taught, saying unto them, Is it not written, My house shall be called of all nations the house of prayer? but ye have made it a den of thieves.

Mark 11:15, 17

He that hasteth to be rich hath an evil eye, and considereth not that poverty shall come upon him.

Proverbs 28:22

For riches are not for ever: and doth the crown endure to every generation?

Proverbs 27:24

For in that day every man shall cast away his idols of silver, and his idols of gold, which your own hands have made unto you for a sin.

Isaiah 31:7

Wherefore if thy hand or thy foot offend thee, cut them off, and cast them from thee: it is better for thee to enter into life halt or maimed, rather than having two hands or two feet to be cast into everlasting fire.

And if thine eye offend thee, pluck it out, and cast it from thee: it is better for thee to enter into life with one eye, rather than having two eyes to be cast into hell fire.

Matthew 18:8-9

But with many of them God was not well pleased: for they were overthrown in the wilderness.

Now these things were our examples, to the intent we should not lust after evil things, as they also lusted.

Neither be ye idolaters, as were some of them; as it is written, The people sat down to eat and drink, and rose up to play.

Neither let us commit fornication, as some of them committed, and fell in one day three and twenty thousand.

I Corinthians 10:5-8

For this ye know, that no whoremonger, nor unclean person, nor covetous man, who is an idolater, hath any inheritance in the kingdom of Christ and of God.

Be not ye therefore partakers with them.

For ye were sometimes darkness, but now are ye light in the Lord; walk as children of light:

(For the fruit of the Spirit is in all goodness and righteousness and truth;)

And be not drunk with wine, wherein is excess; but be filled with the Spirit;

Ephesians 5:5, 7-9, 18

How To Overcome Pride

Pride goeth before destruction, and an haughty spirit before a fall.

Better it is to be of an humble spirit with the lowly, than to divide the spoil with the proud.

He that handleth a matter wisely shall find good: and whoso trusteth in the LORD, happy is he.

Proverbs 16:18-20

He that is of a proud heart stirreth up strife: but he that putteth his trust in the LORD shall be made fat.

He that trusteth in his own heart is a fool: but whoso walketh wisely, he shall be delivered.

Proverbs 28:25-26

And Jesus called a little child unto him, and set him in the midst of them,

And said, Verily I say unto you, Except ye be converted, and become as little children, ye shall not enter into the kingdom of heaven.

Whosoever therefore shall humble himself as this little child, the same is greatest in the kingdom of heaven.

Matthew 18:2-4

But he giveth more grace. Wherefore he saith, God resisteth the proud, but giveth grace unto the humble.

Submit yourselves therefore to God. Resist the devil, and he will flee from you.

Humble yourselves in the sight of the Lord, and he shall lift you up.

James 4:6-7, 10

But it shall not be so among you: but whosoever will be great among you, let him be your minister;

And whosoever will be chief among you, let him be your servant:

Matthew 20:26-27

Likewise, ye younger, submit yourselves unto the elder. Yea, all of you be subject one to another, and be clothed with humility: for God resisteth the proud, and giveth grace to the humble.

Humble yourselves therefore under the mighty hand of God, that he may exalt you in due time:

I Peter 5:5-6

Hear ye, and give ear; be not proud: for the LORD hath spoken.

Give glory to the LORD your God, before he cause darkness, and before your feet stumble upon the dark mountains, and, while ye look for light, he turn it into the shadow of death, and make it gross darkness.

But if ye will not hear it, my soul shall weep in secret places for your pride; and mine eye shall weep sore, and run down with tears, because the LORD's flock is carried away captive.

Jeremiah 13:15-17

Take my yoke upon you, and learn of me; for I am meek and lowly in heart: and ye shall find rest unto your souls.

For my yoke is easy, and my burden is light.

Matthew 11:29-30

The fear of the LORD is the instruction of wisdom; and before honour is humility.

Proverbs 15:33

And whosoever of you will be the chiefest, shall be servant of all.

Mark 10:44

But we have this treasure in earthen vessels, that the excellency of the power may be of God and not of us.

II Corinthians 4:7

But he that glorieth, let him glory in the Lord.

For not he that commendeth himself is approved, but whom the Lord commendeth.

II Corinthians 10:17-18

By humility and the fear of the LORD are riches, and honour, and life.

Proverbs 22:4

Boast not thyself of tomorrow; for thou knowest not what a day may bring forth.

Let another man praise thee, and not thine own mouth; a stranger, and not thine own lips.

Proverbs 27:1-2

A man's pride shall bring him low: but honour shall uphold the humble in spirit.

Proverbs 29:23

Before destruction the heart of man is haughty, and before honour is humility.

Proverbs 18:12

Better is a poor and a wise child than an old and foolish king, who will no more be admonished.

Ecclesiastes 4:13

Not a novice, lest being lifted up with pride he fall into the condemnation of the devil.

Moreover he must have a good report of them which are without; lest he fall into reproach and the snare of the devil.

I Timothy 3:6-7

But he that is greatest among you shall be your servant.

And whosoever shall exalt himself shall be abased; and he that shall humble himself shall be exalted.

Matthew 23:11-12

The Pharisee stood and prayed thus with himself, God, I thank thee, that I am not as other men are, extortioners, unjust, adulterers, or even as this publican.

I fast twice in the week, I give tithes of all that I possess.

And the publican, standing afar off, would not lift up so much as his eyes unto heaven, but smote upon his breast, saying, God be merciful to me a sinner.

I tell you, this man went down to his house justified rather than the other: for every one that exalteth himself shall be abased; and he that humbleth himself shall be exalted.

Luke 18:11-14

Though the LORD be high, yet hath he respect unto the lowly: but the proud he knoweth afar off.

Psalm 138:6

How To Control Your Tongue

Death and life are in the power of the tongue: and they that love it shall eat the fruit thereof.

Proverbs 18:21

Let no corrupt communication proceed out of your mouth, but that which is good to the use of edifying, that it may minister grace unto the hearers.

Let all bitterness, and wrath, and anger, and clamour, and evil speaking, be put away from you, with all malice:

And be ye kind one to another, tenderhearted, forgiving one another, even as God for Christ's sake hath forgiven you.

Ephesians 4:29, 31-32

Pleasant words are as an honeycomb, sweet to the soul, and health to the bones.

Proverbs 16:24

He that keepeth his mouth keepeth his life: but he that openeth wide his lips shall have destruction.

Proverbs 13:3

A good man out of the good treasure of his heart bringeth forth that which is good; and an evil man out of the evil treasure of his heart bringeth forth that which is evil: for of the abundance of the heart his mouth speaketh.

Luke 6:45

But I say unto you, That every idle word that men shall speak, they shall give account thereof in the day of judgment.

Matthew 12:36

Sing unto him, sing psalms unto him, talk ye of all his wondrous works.

I Chronicles 16:9

Whoso keepeth his mouth and his tongue, keepeth his soul from troubles.

Proverbs 21:23

Be not a witness against thy neighbor without cause; and deceive not with thy lips.

Proverbs 24:28

O Timothy, keep that which is committed to thy trust, avoiding profane and vain babblings, and oppositions of science falsely so called:

Which some professing have erred concerning the faith. Grace be with thee. Amen.

I Timothy 6:20-21

But avoid foolish questions, and genealogies, and contentions, and strivings about the law; for they are unprofitable and vain.

Titus 3:9

All the while my breath is in me, and the spirit of God is in my nostrils;

My lips shall not speak wickedness, nor my tongue utter deceit.

Job 27:3-4

But he said unto her, Thou speakest as one of the foolish women speaketh. What? shall we receive good at the hand of God, and shall we not receive evil? In all this did not Job sin with his lips.

Job 2:10

For he that will love life, and see good days, let him refrain his tongue from evil, and his lips that they speak no guile:

I Peter 3:10

But as he which hath called you is holy, so be ye holy in all manner of conversation;

I Peter 1:15

Who, when he was reviled, reviled not again; when he suffered, he threatened not; but committed himself to him that judgeth righteously:

I Peter 2:23

A wholesome tongue is a tree of life: but perverseness therein is a breach in the spirit.

Proverbs 15:4

A fool's mouth is his destruction, and his lips are the snare of his soul.

The words of a talebearer are as wounds, and they go down into the innermost parts of the belly.

Proverbs 18:7-8

And the tongue is a fire, a world of iniquity: so is the tongue among our members, that it defileth the whole body, and setteth on fire the course of nature; and it is set on fire of hell.

Out of the same mouth proceedeth blessing and cursing. My brethren, these things ought not so to be.

Doth a fountain send forth at the same place sweet water and bitter?

James 3:6, 10-11

If any man among you seem to be religious, and bridleth not his tongue, but deceiveth his own heart, this man's religion is vain.

James 1:26

Concerning the works of men, by the word of thy lips I have kept me from the paths of the destroyer.

Psalm 17:4

There is that speaketh like the piercings of a sword: but the tongue of the wise is health.

The lip of truth shall be established for ever: but a lying tongue is but for a moment.

Proverbs 12:18-19

Set a watch, O LORD, before my mouth; keep the door of my lips.

Psalm 141:3

There is gold, and a multitude of rubies: but the lips of knowledge are a precious jewel.

Proverbs 20:15

Whoso offereth praise glorifieth me: and to him that ordereth his conversation aright will I shew the salvation of God.

Psalm 50:23

How To Be Christ-Centered

Let the word of Christ dwell in you richly in all wisdom; teaching and admonishing one another in psalms and hymns and spiritual songs, singing with grace in your hearts to the Lord.

And whatsoever ye do in word or deed, do all in the name of the Lord Jesus, giving thanks to God and the Father by him.

Colossians 3:16-17

I love them that love me; and those that seek me early shall find me.

Proverbs 8:17

Seek the LORD and his strength, seek his face continually.

Remember his marvellous works that he hath done, his wonders, and the judgments of his mouth;

I Chronicles 16:11-12

Ye are my friends, if ye do whatsoever I command you.

Henceforth I call you not servants; for the servant knoweth not what his lord doeth: but I have called you friends; for all things that I have heard of my Father I have made known unto you.

Ye have not chosen me, but I have chosen you, and ordained you, that ye should go and bring forth fruit, and that your fruit should remain: that whatsoever ye shall ask of the Father in my name, he may give it you.

John 15:14-16

Speaking to yourselves in psalms and hymns and spiritual songs, singing and making melody in your heart to the Lord;

Giving thanks always for all things unto God and the Father in the name of our Lord Jesus Christ;

Ephesians 5:19-20

I WILL bless the LORD at all times: his praise shall continually be in my mouth.

My soul shall make her boast in the LORD: the humble shall hear thereof, and be glad.

O magnify the LORD with me, and let us exalt his name together.

I sought the LORD, and he heard me, and delivered me from all my fears.

Psalm 34:1-4

O GOD, thou art my God; early will I seek thee: my soul thirsteth for thee, my flesh longeth for thee in a dry and thirsty land, where no water is;

To see thy power and thy glory, so as I have seen thee in the sanctuary.

My soul shall be satisfied as with marrow and fatness; and my mouth shall praise thee with joyful lips:

When I remember thee upon my bed, and meditate on thee in the night watches.

Because thou hast been my help, therefore in the shadow of thy wings will I rejoice.

Psalms 63:1-2, 5-7

But put ye on the Lord Jesus Christ, and make not provision for the flesh, to fulfil the lusts thereof.

Romans 13:14

So will I sing praise unto thy name for ever, that I may daily perform my vows.

Psalm 61:8

IN thee, O LORD, do I put my trust: let me never be put to confusion.

For thou art my hope, O Lord GOD: thou art my trust from my youth.

Let my mouth be filled with thy praise and with thy honour all the day.

Psalm 71:1, 5, 8

Trust in him at all times; ye people, pour out your heart before him: God is a refuge for us. Selah.

Psalm 62:8

Let them shout for joy, and be glad, that favour my righteous cause: yea, let them say continually, Let the LORD be magnified, which hath pleasure in the prosperity of his servant.

And my tongue shall speak of thy righteousness and of thy praise all the day long.

Psalm 35:27-28

IT is a good thing to give thanks unto the LORD, and to sing praises unto thy name, O most High:

To shew forth thy lovingkindness in the morning and thy faithfulness every night,

For thou, LORD, hast made me glad through thy work: I will triumph in the works of thy hands.

Psalm 92:1-2, 4

Sing unto the LORD, bless his name; shew forth his salvation from day to day.

Psalm 96:2

From the rising of the sun unto the going down of the same the LORD's name is to be praised.

Psalm 113:3

I will delight myself in thy statutes: I will not forget thy word.

Make me to understand the way of thy precepts: so shall I talk of thy wondrous works.

Psalm 119:16, 27

My soul waiteth for the Lord more than they that watch for the morning: I say, more than they that watch for the morning.

Let Israel hope in the LORD: for with the LORD there is mercy, and with him is plenteous redemption.

Psalm 130:6-7

I will sing unto the LORD as long as I live: I will sing praise to my God while I have my being.

My meditation of him shall be sweet: I will be glad in the LORD.

Psalm 104:33-34

By him therefore let us offer the sacrifice of praise to God continually, that is, the fruit of our lips giving thanks to his name.

Hebrews 13:15

Thou wilt keep him in perfect peace, whose mind is stayed on thee: because he trusteth in thee.

Isaiah 26:3

And he said to them all, If any man will come after me, let him deny himself, and take up his cross daily, and follow me.

For whosoever will save his life shall lose it: but whosoever will lose his life for my sake, the same shall save it.

For what is a man advantaged, if he gain the whole world, and lose himself, or be cast away?

Luke 9:23-25

Be merciful unto me, O Lord: for I cry unto thee daily.

Rejoice the soul of thy servant: for unto thee, O Lord, do I lift up my soul.

For thou, Lord, art good, and ready to forgive; and plenteous in mercy unto all them that call upon thee.

Psalm 86:3-5

For in him we live, and move, and have our being; as certain also of your own poets have said, For we are also his offspring.

Acts 17:28

How To Understand The Liberty That Is In Christ

THERE is therefore now no condemnation to them which are in Christ Jesus, who walk not after the flesh, but after the Spirit.

For the law of the Spirit of life in Christ Jesus hath made me free from the law of sin and death.

Romans 8:1-2

For, brethren, ye have been called unto liberty; only use not liberty for an occasion to the flesh, but by love serve one another.

Galatians 5:13

There is neither Jew nor Greek, there is neither bond nor free, there is neither male nor female: for ye are all one in Christ Jesus.

Galatians 3:28

But whoso looketh into the perfect law of liberty, and continueth therein, he being not a forgetful hearer, but a doer of the work, this man shall be blessed in his deed.

James 1:25

I Jesus have sent mine angel to testify unto you these things in the churches. I am the root and the offspring of David, and the bright and morning star.

And the Spirit and the bride say, Come. And let him that heareth say, Come. And let him that is athirst come. And whosoever will, let him take the water of life freely.

Revelation 22:16-17

And ye shall know the truth, and the truth shall make you free.

If the Son therefore shall make you free, ye shall be free indeed.

John 8:32, 36

Now the Lord is that Spirit: and where the Spirit of the Lord is, there is liberty.

II Corinthians 3:17

STAND fast therefore in the liberty wherewith Christ hath made us free, and be not entangled again with the yoke of bondage.

Galatians 5:1

Because the creature itself also shall be delivered from the bondage of corruption into the glorious liberty of the children of God.

Romans 8:21

AM I not an apostle? am I not free? have I not seen Jesus Christ our Lord? are not ye my work in the Lord?

I Corinthians 9:1

As free, and not using your liberty for a cloak of maliciousness, but as the servants of God.

I Peter 2:16

Even the righteousness of God which is by faith of Jesus Christ unto all and upon all them that believe: for there is no difference:

For all have sinned, and come short of the glory of God;

Being justified freely by his grace through the redemption that is in Christ Jesus:

Whom God hath set forth to be a propitiation through faith in his blood, to declare his righteousness for the remission of sins that are past, through the forbearance of God;

Romans 3:22-25

For thus saith the LORD, ye have sold yourselves for nought; and ye shall be redeemed without money.

Isaiah 52:3

For though I be free from all men, yet have I made myself servant unto all,that I might gain the more.

I Corinthians 9:19

How To Praise The Lord

Because thy lovingkindness is better than life, my lips shall praise thee.

Thus will I bless thee while I live: I will lift up my hands in thy name.

My soul shall be satisfied as with marrow and fatness; and my mouth shall praise thee with joyful lips:

Psalm 63:3-5

PRAISE ye the LORD. Sing unto the LORD a new song, and his praise in the congregation of saints.

Let Israel rejoice in him that made him: let the children of Zion be joyful in their King.

Let them praise his name in the dance: let them sing praises unto him with the timbrel and harp.

For the LORD taketh pleasure in his people: he will beautify the meek with salvation.

Let the saints be joyful in glory: let them sing aloud upon their beds.

Let the high praises of God be in their mouth, and a two-edged sword in their hand;

Psalm 149:1-6

PRAISE ye the LORD. Praise God in his sanctuary: praise him in the firmament of his power.

Praise him for his mighty acts: praise him according to his excellent greatness.

Praise him with the sound of the trumpet: praise him with the psaltery and harp.

Praise him with the timbrel and dance: praise him with stringed instruments and organs.

Praise him upon the loud cymbals; praise him upon the high sounding cymbals.

Let every thing that hath breath praise the Lord. Praise ye the LORD.

Psalm 150:1-6

I WILL bless the LORD at all times: his praise shall continually be in my mouth.

Psalm 34:1

PRAISE ye the LORD. Praise, O ye servants of the LORD, praise the name of the LORD.

Blessed be the name of the LORD from this time forth and for evermore.

From the rising of the sun unto the going down of the same the LORD'S name is to be praised.

Psalm 113:1-3

Whoso offereth praise glorifieth me: and to him that ordereth his conversation aright will I shew the salvation of God.

Psalm 50:23

Let your conversation be without covetousness; and be content with such things as ye have: for he hath said, I will never leave thee, nor forsake thee.

Hebrews 13:5

The voice of joy, and the voice of gladness, the voice of the bridegroom, and the voice of the bride, the voice of them that shall say Praise the LORD of hosts; for the LORD is good; for his mercy endureth for ever: and of them that shall bring the sacrifice of praise into the house of the LORD. For I will cause to return the captivity of the land, as at the first, saith the LORD.

Jeremiah 33:11

But ye are a chosen generation, a royal priesthood, an holy nation, a peculiar people; that ye should shew forth the praises of him who hath called you out of darkness into his marvellous light:

I Peter 2:9

Accept, I beseech thee, the freewill offerings of my mouth, O LORD, and teach me thy judgments.

Psalm 119:108

And at midnight Paul and Silas prayed, and sang praises unto God: and the prisoners heard them.

Acts 16:25

PRAISE ye the LORD. Praise the LORD, O my soul.

While I live will I praise the LORD: I will sing praises unto my God while I have any being.

Psalm 146:1-2

Oh that men would praise the LORD for his goodness, and for his wonderful works to the children of men!

And let them sacrifice the sacrifices of thanksgiving, and declare his works with rejoicing.

Psalm 107:21, 22

My heart is fixed, O GOD, my heart is fixed: I will sing and give praise.

Awake up, my glory; awake, psaltery and harp: I myself will awake early.

I will praise thee, O LORD, among the people: I will sing unto thee among the nations.

Psalm 57:7-9

GREAT is the LORD, and greatly to be praised in the city of our God, in the mountain of his holiness.

Psalm 48:1

But thou art holy, O thou that inhabitest the praises of Israel.

Our fathers trusted in thee: they trusted, and thou didst deliver them.

Psalm 22:3, 4

I will praise the name of God with a song, and will magnify him with thanksgiving.

Psalm 69:30

He that believeth on me, as the scripture hath said, out of his belly shall flow rivers of living water.

John 7:38

How To Have The Joy Of The Lord

His lord said unto him, Well done, thou good and faithful servant: thou hast been faithful over a few things, I will make thee ruler over many things: enter thou into the joy of thy lord.

Matthew 25:21

These things have I spoken unto you, that my joy might remain in you, and that your joy might be full.

This is my commandment, That ye love one another, as I have loved you.

John 15:11-12

But let all those that put their trust in thee rejoice: let them ever shout for joy, because thou defendest them: let them also that love thy name be joyful in thee.

For thou, LORD, wilt bless the righteous; with favour wilt thou compass him as with a shield.

Psalm 5:11-12

Come unto me, all ye that labour and are heavy laden, and I will give you rest.

Take my yoke upon you, and learn of me; for I am meek and lowly in heart: and ye shall find rest unto your souls.

For my yoke is easy, and my burden is light.

Matthew 11:28-30

For God hath not given us the spirit of fear; but of power, and of love, and of a sound mind.

II Timothy 1:7

For the kingdom of God is not meat and drink; but righteousness, and peace, and joy in the Holy Ghost.

For he that in these things serveth Christ is acceptable to God, and approved of men.

Romans 14:17-18

A merry heart doeth good like a medicine: but a broken spirit drieth the bones.

Proverbs 17:22

Notwithstanding in this rejoice not, that the spirits are subject unto you; but rather rejoice, because your names are written in heaven.

In that hour Jesus rejoiced in spirit, and said, I thank thee, O Father, Lord of heaven and earth, that thou has hid these things from the wise and prudent, and hast revealed them unto babes: even so, Father; for so it seemed good in thy sight.

Luke 10:20-21

Thou lovest righteousness, and hatest wickedness: therefore God, thy God, hath anointed thee with the oil of gladness above thy fellows.

All thy garments smell of myrrh, and aloes, and cassia, out of the ivory palaces, whereby they have made thee glad.

Psalm 45:7-8

A merry heart maketh a cheerful countenance: but by sorrow of the heart the spirit is broken.

Proverbs 15:13

And ye became followers of us, and of the Lord, having received the word in much affliction, with joy of the Holy Ghost:

I Thessalonians 1:6

Restore unto me the joy of thy salvation; and uphold me with thy free spirit.

Then will I teach transgressors thy ways; and sinners shall be converted unto thee.

Psalm 51:12-13

Let the saints be joyful in glory: let them sing aloud upon their beds.

Psalm 149:5

This is the day which the LORD hath made; we will rejoice and be glad in it.

Psalm 118:24

They that sow in tears shall reap in joy.
He that goeth forth and weepeth, bearing precious seed, shall doubtless come again with rejoicing, bringing his sheaves with him.

Psalm 126:5-6

. . . for this day is holy unto our LORD: neither be ye sorry, for the joy of the LORD is your strength.

Nehemiah 8:10b

Maturing In Christ...

How To Handle Spiritual Trials

Beloved, think it not strange concerning the fiery trial which is to try you, as though some strange thing happened unto you:

But rejoice, inasmuch as ye are partakers of Christ's sufferings; that, when his glory shall be revealed, ye may be glad also with exceeding joy.

Yet if any man suffer as a Christian, let him not be ashamed; but let him glorify God on this behalf.

I Peter 4:12-13, 16

When thou passest through the waters, I will be with thee; and through the rivers, they shall not overflow thee: when thou walkest through the fire, thou shalt not be burned; neither shall the flame kindle upon thee.

For I am the LORD thy God, the Holy One of Israel, thy saviour: I gave Egypt for thy ransom, Ethiopia and Seba for thee.

Isaiah 43:2-3

Deliver me out of the mire, and let me not sink: let me be delivered from them that hate me, and out of the deep waters.

Let not the waterflood overflow me, neither let the deep swallow me up, and let not the pit shut her mouth upon me.

Hear me, O LORD; for thy lovingkindness is good: turn unto me according to the multitude of thy tender mercies.

And hide not thy face from thy servant; for I am in trouble: hear me speedily.

Draw nigh unto my soul, and redeem it: deliver me because of mine enemies.

Psalm 69:14-18

In thee, O LORD, do I put my trust; let me never be ashamed: deliver me in thy righteousness.

Bow down thine ear to me; deliver me speedily: be thou my strong rock, for an house of defence to save me.

For thou art my rock and my fortress; therefore for thy name's sake lead me, and guide me.

Pull me out of the net that they have laid privily for me: for thou art my strength.

Into thine hand I commit my spirit: thou hast redeemed me, O LORD God of truth.

I will be glad and rejoice in thy mercy: for thou hast considered my trouble; thou hast known my soul in adversities;

And hast not shut me up into the hand of the enemy: thou hast set my feet in a large room.

Psalm 31:1-5, 7-8

The righteous cry, and the LORD heareth, and delivereth them out of all their troubles.

The LORD is nigh unto them that are of a broken heart; and saveth such as be of a contrite spirit.

Many are the afflictions of the righteous: but the LORD delivereth him out of them all.

Psalm 34:17-19

For thou wilt light my candle: the LORD my God will enlighten my darkness.

For by thee I have run through a troop; and by my God have I leaped over a wall.

As for God, his way is perfect: the word of the LORD is tried: he is a buckler to all those that trust in him.

It is God that girdeth me with strength, and maketh my way perfect.

Psalm 18:28-30, 32

Why art thou cast down, O my soul? And why art thou disquieted within me? hope in God: for I shall yet praise him, who is the health of my countenance, and my God.

Psalm 43:5

All this is come upon us; yet have we not forgotten thee, neither have we dealt falsely in thy covenant.

Our heart is not turned back, neither have our steps declined from thy way;

Though thou hast sore broken us in the place of dragons, and covered us with the shadow of death.

If we have forgotten the name of our God, or stretched out our hands to a strange god;

Shall not God search this out? for he knoweth the secrets of the heart.

Psalm 44:17-21

Cast thy burden upon the LORD, and he shall sustain thee: he shall never suffer the righteous to be moved.

Psalm 55:22

Create in me a clean heart, O God; and renew a right spirit within me.

Cast me not away from thy presence; and take not thy holy spirit from me.

Restore unto me the joy of thy salvation; and uphold me with thy free spirit.

The sacrifices of God are a broken spirit: a broken and a contrite heart, O God, thou wilt not despise.

Psalm 51:10-12, 17

Give us help from trouble: for vain is the help of man.

Through God we shall do valiantly: for he it is that shall tread down our enemies.

Psalm 60:11-12

In God have I put my trust: I will not be afraid what man can do unto me.

Thy vows are upon me, O God: I will render praises unto thee.

For thou hast delivered my soul from death: wilt not thou deliver my feet from falling, that I may walk before God in the light of the living?

Psalm 56:11-13

I will extol thee, O LORD; for thou hast lifted me up, and hast not made my foes to rejoice over me.

O LORD my God, I cried unto thee, and thou hast healed me.

O LORD, thou hast brought up my soul from the grave: thou hast kept me alive, that I should not go down to the pit.

Sing unto the LORD, O ye saints of his, and give thanks at the remembrance of his holiness.

For his anger endureth but a moment; in his favour is life: weeping may endure for a night, but joy cometh in the morning.

Psalm 30:1-5

The LORD hath chastened me sore: but he hath not given me over unto death.

Open to me the gates of righteousness: I will go into them, and I will praise the LORD:

This gate of the LORD, into which the righteous shall enter.

I will praise thee: for thou hast heard me, and art become my salvation.

Psalm 118:18-21

It is good for me that I have been afflicted; that I might learn thy statutes.

Let, I pray thee, thy merciful kindness be for my comfort, according to thy word unto thy servant.

Let thy tender mercies come unto me, that I may live: for thy law is my delight.

Psalm 119:71, 76-77

Blessed is the man that endureth temptation: for when he is tried, he shall receive the crown of life, which the Lord hath promised to them that love him.

For he beholdeth himself, and goeth his way, and straightway forgetteth what manner of man he was.

James 1:12, 24

Then Job arose, and rent his mantle, and shaved his head, and fell down upon the ground, and worshipped,

And said, Naked came I out of my mother's womb, and naked shall I return thither: the LORD gave, and the LORD hath taken away; blessed be the name of the LORD.

In all this Job sinned not, nor charged God foolishly.

Job 1:20-22

Though he slay me, yet will I trust in him: but I will maintain mine own ways before him.

He also shall be my salvation: for an hypocrite shall not come before him.

Job 13:15-16

But he knoweth the way that I take: when he hath tried me, I shall come forth as gold.

My foot hath held his steps, his way have I kept, and not declined.

Job 23:10-11

How To Face Serious Illness

Is any sick among you? let him call for the elders of the church; and let them pray over him, anointing him with oil in the name of the Lord:

And the prayer of faith shall save the sick, and the Lord shall raise him up; and if he have committed sins, they shall be forgiven him.

James 5:14-15

Thou wilt keep him in perfect peace, whose mind is stayed on thee: because he trusteth in thee.

Trust ye in the LORD for ever: for in the LORD JEHOVAH is everlasting strength:

Isaiah 26:3-4

Heal me, O LORD, and I shall be healed; save me, and I shall be saved: for thou art my praise.

Jeremiah 17:14

For all things are for your sakes, that the abundant grace might through the thanksgiving of many redound to the glory of God.

For which cause we faint not; but though our outward man perish, yet the inward man is renewed day by day.

For our light affliction, which is but for a moment, worketh for us a far more exceeding and eternal weight of glory;

While we look not at the things which are seen, but at the things which are not seen: for the things which are seen are temporal; but the things which are not seen are eternal.

II Corinthians 4:15-18

And I said, This is my infirmity: but I will remember the years of the right hand of the most high.

I will remember the works of the LORD: surely I will remember thy wonders of old.

I will meditate also of all thy work, and talk of thy doings.

Thy way, O God, is in the sanctuary: who is so great a God as our God?

Thou art the God that doest wonders: thou hast declared thy strength among the people.

Psalm 77:10-14

Yea, though I walk through the valley of the shadow of death, I will fear no evil: for thou art with me; thy rod and thy staff they comfort me.

Psalm 23:4

And behold, a woman, which was diseased with an issue of blood twelve years, came behind him, and touched the hem of his garment:

For she said within herself, If I may but touch his garment, I shall be whole.

But Jesus turned him about, and when he saw her, he said, Daughter, be of good comfort; thy faith hath made thee whole. And the woman was made whole from that hour.

Matthew 9:20-22

For this God is our God for ever and ever: he will be our guide even unto death.

Psalm 48:14

I call to remembrance my song in the night: I commune with mine own heart: and my spirit made diligent search.

Psalm 77:6

But God will redeem my soul from the power of the grave: for he shall receive me. Selah.

Psalm 49:15

In those days was Hezekiah sick unto death. And the prophet Isaiah the son of Amoz came to him, and said unto him, Thus saith the LORD, Set thine house in order; for thou shalt die, and not live.

Then he turned his face to the wall, and prayed unto the LORD saying,

I beseech thee, O LORD, remember now how I have walked before thee in truth and with a perfect heart, and have done that which is good in thy sight. And Hezekiah wept sore.

And it came to pass, afore Isaiah was gone out into the middle court, that the word of the LORD came to him saying,

Turn again, and tell Hezekiah the captain of my people, Thus saith the LORD, the God of David thy father, I have heard thy prayer, I have seen thy tears: behold, I will heal thee: on the third day thou shalt go up unto the house of the LORD.

And I will add unto thy days fifteen years; and I will deliver thee and this city out of the hand of the king of Assyria; and I will defend this city for mine own sake, and for my servant David's sake.

And Isaiah said, Take a lump of figs. And they took and laid it on the boil, and he recovered.

II Kings 20:1-7

Who his own self bare our sins in his own body on the tree, that we, being dead to sins, should live unto righteousness: by whose stripes ye were healed.

I Peter 2:24

FOR we know that if our earthly house of this tabernacle were dissolved, we have a building of God, an house not made with hands, eternal in the heavens.

II Corinthians 5:1

I will sing unto the LORD as long as I live: I will sing praise to my God while I have my being.

My meditation of him shall be sweet: I will be glad in the LORD.

Psalm 104:33-34

While I live will I praise the LORD: I will sing praises unto my god while I have any being.

Psalm 146:2

And a certain man lame from his mother's womb was carried, whom they laid daily at the gate of the temple which is called Beautiful, to ask alms of them that entered into the temple;

Who seeing Peter and John about to go into the temple asked an alms.

And Peter, fastening his eyes upon him with John, said, Look on us.

And he gave heed unto them, expecting to receive something of them.

Then Peter said, Silver and gold have I none; but such as I have give I thee: In the name of Jesus Christ of Nazareth rise up and walk.

And he took him by the right hand, and lifted him up: and immediately his feet and ankle bones received strength.

And he leaping up stood, and walked, and entered with them into the temple, walking, and leaping, and praising God.

Acts 3:2-8

How To Handle Suffering

Forasmuch then as Christ hath suffered for us in the flesh, arm yourselves likewise with the same mind: for he that hath suffered in the flesh hath ceased from sin;

That he no longer should live the rest of his time in the flesh to the lusts of men, but to the will of God.

Beloved, think it not strange concerning the fiery trial which is to try you, as though some strange thing happened unto you:

But rejoice, inasmuch as ye are partakers of Christ's sufferings; that, when his glory shall be revealed, ye may be glad also with exceeding joy.

If ye be reproached for the name of Christ, happy are ye; for the spirit of glory and of God resteth upon you: on their part he is evil spoken of, but on your part he is glorified.

But let none of you suffer as a murderer, or as a thief, or as an evildoer, or as a busybody in other men's matters.

Yet if any man suffer as a Christian, let him not be ashamed; but let him glorify God on this behalf.

For the time is come that judgment must begin at the house of God: and if it first begin at us, what shall the end be of them that obey not the gospel of God?

I Peter 4:1-2, 12-17

The righteous cry, and the LORD heareth, and delivereth them out of all their troubles.

The LORD is nigh unto them that are of a broken heart; and saveth such as be of a contrite spirit.

Many are the afflictions of the righteous: but the LORD delivereth him out of them all.

Psalm 34:17-19

For whom the Lord loveth he chasteneth, and scourgeth every son whom he receiveth.

If ye endure chastening, God dealeth with you as with sons; for what son is he whom the father chasteneth not?

But if ye be without chastisement, whereof all are partakers, then are ye bastards, and not sons.

Now no chastening for the present seemeth to be joyous, but grievous: nevertheless afterward it yieldeth the peaceable fruit of righteousness unto them which are exercised thereby.

Wherefore lift up the hands which hang down, and the feeble knees;

And make straight paths for your feet, lest that which is lame be turned out of the way; but let it rather be healed.

Hebrews 12:6-8, 11-13

We are troubled on every side, yet not distressed; we are perplexed, but not in despair;

Persecuted, but not forsaken; cast down, but not destroyed;

Always bearing about in the body the dying of the Lord Jesus, that the life also of Jesus might be made manifest in our body.

For our light affliction, which is but for a moment, worketh for us a far more exceeding and eternal weight of glory;

While we look not at the things which are seen, but at the things which are not seen: for the things which are seen are temporal; but the things which are not seen are eternal.

II Corinthians 4:8-10, 17-18

But the God of all grace, who hath called us into his eternal glory by Christ Jesus, after that ye have suffered a while, make you perfect, stablish, strengthen, settle you.

To him be glory and dominion for ever and ever. Amen.

I Peter 5:10-11

For what glory is it, if, when ye be buffeted for your faults, ye shall take it patiently? but if, when ye do well, and suffer for it, ye take it patiently, this is acceptable with God.

For even hereunto were ye called: because Christ also suffered for us, leaving us an example, that ye should follow his steps:

I Peter 2:20-21

And if children, then heirs; heirs of God, and joint-heirs with Christ; if so be that we suffer with him, that we may be also glorified together.

For I reckon that the sufferings of this present time are not worthy to be compared with the glory which shall be revealed in us.

Romans 8:17-18

Thou therefore endure hardness, as a good soldier of Jesus Christ.

II Timothy 2:3

But we see Jesus, who was made a little lower than the angels for the suffering of death, crowned with glory and honour; that he by the grace of God should taste death for every man.

For it became him, for whom are all things, and by whom are all things, in bringing many sons unto glory, to make the captain of their salvation perfect through sufferings.

Hebrews 2:9-10

Though he were a Son, yet learned he obedience by the things which he suffered;

And being made perfect, he became the author of eternal salvation unto all them that obey him;

Hebrews 5:8-9

Blessed is the man that endureth temptation: for when he is tried, he shall receive the crown of life, which the Lord hath promised to them that love him.

James 1:12

I know both how to be abased, and I know how to abound: every where and in all things I am instructed both to be full and to be hungry, both to abound and to suffer need.

I can do all things through Christ which strengtheneth me.

Philippians 4:12-13

Be not thou therefore ashamed of the testimony of our Lord, nor of me his prisoner: but be thou partaker of the afflictions of the gospel according to the power of God;

For the which cause I also suffer these things: nevertheless I am not ashamed: for I know whom I have believed, and am persuaded that he is able to keep that which I have committed unto him against that day.

II Timothy 1:8, 12

It is a faithful saying: For if we be dead with him, we shall also live with him:

If we suffer, we shall also reign with him; if we deny him, he also will deny us:

II Timothy 2:11-12

Take, my brethren, the prophets, who have spoken in the name of the Lord, for an example of suffering affliction, and of patience.

Behold, we count them happy which endure. Ye have heard of the patience of Job, and have seen the end of the Lord; that the Lord is very pitiful, and of tender mercy.

James 5:10-11

Wherefore let them that suffer according to the will of God commit the keeping of their souls to him in well-doing, as unto a faithful Creator.

I Peter 4:19

How To Survive Financial Problems

For the love of money is the root of all evil: which while some coveted after, they have erred from the faith, and pierced themselves through with many sorrows.

But thou, O man of God, flee these things; and follow after righteousness, godliness, faith, love, patience, meekness.

I Timothy 6:10-11

Not that I speak in respect of want: for I have learned in whatsoever state I am, therewith to be content.

I know both how to be abased, and I know how to abound: every where and in all things I am instructed both to be full and to be hungry, both to abound and to suffer need.

I can do all things through Christ which strengtheneth me.

Philippians 4:11-13

Therefore take not thought, saying, What shall we eat? or, What shall we drink? or, Wherewithal shall we be clothed?

(For after all these things do the Gentiles seek:) for your heavenly Father knoweth that ye have need of all these things.

But seek ye first the kingdom of God, and his righteousness; and all these things shall be added unto you.

Take therefore no thought for the morrow: for the morrow shall take thought for the things of itself. Sufficient unto the day is the evil thereof.

Matthew 6:31-34

Trust in the LORD, and do good; so shalt thou dwell in the land, and verily thou shalt be fed.

Delight thyself also in the LORD: and he shall give thee the desires of thine heart.

Psalm 37:3-4

Charge them that are rich in this world, that they be not high-minded, nor trust in uncertain riches, but in the living God, who giveth us richly all things to enjoy;

That they do good, that they be rich in good works, ready to distribute, willing to communicate;

Laying up in store for themselves a good foundation against the time to come, that they may lay hold on eternal life.

I Timothy 6:17-19

This poor man cried, and the LORD heard him, and saved him out of all his troubles.

The angel of the LORD encampeth round about them that fear him, and delivereth them.

O taste and see that the LORD is good: blessed is the man that trusteth in him.

O fear the LORD, ye his saints: for there is no want to them that fear him.

The young lions do lack, and suffer hunger: but they that seek the LORD shall not want any good thing.

Psalm 34:6-10

And the Lord said, Who then is that faithful and wise steward, whom his lord shall make ruler over his household, to give them their portion of meat in due season?

Blessed is that servant, whom his lord when he cometh shall find so doing.

Of a truth I say unto you, that he will make him ruler over all that he hath.

Luke 12:42-44

If then God so clothe the grass, which is to-day in the field, and to-morrow is cast into the oven; how much more will he clothe you, O ye of little faith?

And seek not ye what ye shall eat, or what ye shall drink, neither be ye of doubtful mind.

For all these things do the nations of the world seek after: and your Father knoweth that ye have need of these things.

But rather seek ye the kingdom of God; and all these things shall be added unto you.

Luke 12:28-31

And when he had fasted forty days and forty nights, he was afterward an hungered.

And when the tempter came to him, he said, If thou be the Son of God, command that these stones be made bread.

But he answered and said, It is written, Man shall not live by bread alone, but by every word that proceedeth out of the mouth of God.

Matthew 4:2-4

I have been young, and now am old; yet have I not seen the righteous forsaken, nor his seed begging bread.

He is ever merciful, and lendeth; and his seed is blessed.

Psalm 37:25-26

They wandered in the wilderness in a solitary way; they found no city to dwell in.

Hungry and thirsty, their soul fainted in them.

Then they cried unto the LORD in their trouble, and he delivered them out of their distresses.

And he led them forth by the right way, that they might go to a city of habitation.

Oh that men would praise the LORD for his goodness, and for his wonderful works to the children of men!

Psalm 107:4-8

Pray for the peace of Jerusalem: they shall prosper that love thee.

Psalm 122:6

The LORD also will be a refuge for the oppressed, a refuge in times of trouble.

And they that know thy name will put their trust in thee: for thou, LORD, hast not forsaken them that seek thee.

Psalm 9:9-10

And he said unto them, Take heed, and beware of covetousness: for a man's life consisteth not in the abundance of the things which he possesseth.

Luke 12:15

So that we may boldly say, The Lord is my helper, and I will not fear what man shall do unto me.

Hebrews 13:6

And he said unto his disciples, Therefore I say unto you, Take no thought for your life, what ye shall eat; neither for the body, what ye shall put on.

The life is more than meat, and the body is more than raiment.

Consider the ravens: for they neither sow nor reap; which neither have storehouse nor barn; and God feedeth them: how much more are ye better than the fowls?

Luke 12:22-24

But my God shall supply all your need according to his riches in glory by Christ Jesus.

Philippians 4:19

For ye have need of patience, that, after ye have done the will of God, ye might receive the promise.

Hebrews 10:36

He that trusteth in his riches shall fall: but the righteous shall flourish as a branch.

Proverbs 11:28

There is that maketh himself rich, yet hath nothing: there is that maketh himself poor, yet hath great riches.

Wealth gotten by vanity shall be diminished: but he that gathereth by labour shall increase.

Proverbs 13:7, 11

Remove far from me vanity and lies: give me neither poverty nor riches; feed me with food convenient for me:

Proverbs 30:8

Hearken, my beloved brethren, Hath not God chosen the poor of this world rich in faith, and heirs of the kingdom which he hath promised to them that love him?

James 2:5

How To Handle Stress

Peace I leave with you, my peace I give unto you: not as the world giveth, give I unto you. Let not your heart be troubled, neither let it be afraid.

John 14:27

Be careful for nothing; but in everything by prayer and supplication with thanksgiving let your requests be made known unto God.

And the peace of God, which passeth all understanding, shall keep your hearts and minds through Christ Jesus.

Finally, brethren, whatsoever things are true, whatsoever things are honest, whatsoever things are just, whatsoever things are pure, whatsoever things are lovely, whatsoever things are of good report; if there be any virtue, and if there be any praise, think on these things.

Philippians 4:6-8

Fear thou not; for I am with thee: be not dismayed; for I am thy God: I will strengthen thee; yea, I will help thee; yea, I will uphold thee with the right hand of my righteousness.

Isaiah 41:10

He maketh me to lie down in green pastures: he leadeth me beside the still waters.

He restoreth my soul: he leadeth me in the paths of righteousness for his name's sake.

Yea, though I walk through the valley of the shadow of death, I will fear no evil: for thou art with me; thy rod and thy staff they comfort me.

Psalm 23:2-4

Casting all your care upon him; for he careth for you.

Be sober, be vigilant; because your adversary the devil, as a roaring lion, walketh about, seeking whom he may devour:

Whom resist steadfast in the faith, knowing that the same afflictions are accomplished in your brethren that are in the world.

But the God of all grace, who hath called us unto his eternal glory by Christ Jesus, after that ye have suffered a while, make you perfect, stablish, strengthen, settle you.

To him be glory and dominion for ever and ever. Amen.

I Peter 5:7-11

He shall not be afraid of evil tidings: his heart is fixed, trusting in the LORD.

His heart is established, he shall not be afraid, until he sees his desire upon his enemies.

Psalm 112:7-8

GOD is our refuge and strength, a very present help in trouble.

Therefore will not we fear, though the earth be removed, and though the mountains be carried into the midst of the sea;

Though the waters thereof roar and be troubled, though the mountains shake with the swelling thereof. Selah.

Psalm 46:1-3

What time I am afraid, I will trust in thee.

In God I will praise his word, in God I have put my trust; I will not fear what flesh can do unto me.

Thou tellest my wanderings: put thou my tears into thy bottle: are they not in thy book?

When I cry unto thee, then shall mine enemies turn back: this I know; for God is for me.

Psalm 56: 3-4, 8-9

Surely he shall deliver thee from the snare of the fowler, and from the noisome pestilence.

He shall cover thee with his feathers, and under his wings shalt thou trust: his truth shall be thy shield and buckler.

Thou shalt not be afraid for the terror by night; nor for the arrow that flieth by day;

Nor for the pestilence that walketh in darkness; nor for the destruction that wasteth at noon-day.

A thousand shall fall at thy side, and ten thousand at thy right hand, but it shall not come nigh thee.

Psalm 91:3-7

Hungry and thirsty, their soul fainted in them.

Then they cried unto the LORD in their trouble, and he delivered them out of their distresses.

And he led them forth by the right way, that they might go to a city of habitation.

Psalm 107:5-7

The LORD shall preserve thee from all evil: he shall preserve thy soul.

The LORD shall preserve thy going out and thy coming in from this time forth, and even for evermore.

Psalm 121:7-8

And he was in the hinder part of the ship, asleep on a pillow: and they awake him, and say unto him, Master, carest thou not that we perish?

And he arose, and rebuked the wind, and said unto the sea, Peace, be still. And the wind ceased, and there was a great calm.

And he said unto them, Why are ye so fearful? how is it that ye have no faith?

Mark 4:38-40

Be ye angry, and sin not: let not the sun go down upon your wrath:

Neither give place to the devil.

Ephesians 4:26-27

But thou, O LORD, art a shield for me; my glory, and the lifter up of mine head.

I cried unto the LORD with my voice, and he heard me out of his holy hill. Selah.

I will not be afraid of ten thousands of people, that have set themselves against me round about.

Psalm 3:3, 4, 6

Therefore take no thought, saying, What shall we eat? or, What shall we drink? or, Wherewithal shall we be clothed?

(For after all these things do the Gentiles seek:) for your heavenly Father knoweth that ye have need of all these things.

But seek ye first the kingdom of God, and his righteousness; and all these things shall be added unto you.

Take therefore no thought for the morrow: for the morrow shall take thought for the things of itself. Sufficient unto the day is the evil thereof.

Matthew 6:31-34

Thou wilt keep him in perfect peace, whose mind is stayed on thee: because he trusteth in thee.

Trust ye in the LORD for ever: for in the LORD JEHOVAH is everlasting strength:

Isaiah 26:3-4

For God hath not given us the spirit of fear; but of power, and of love, and of a sound mind.

Who hath saved us, and called us with an holy calling, not according to our works, but according to his own purpose and grace, which was given us in Christ Jesus before the world began,

II Timothy 1:7, 9

Come unto me, all ye that labour and are heavy laden, and I will give you rest.

Take my yoke upon you, and learn of me; for I am meek and lowly in heart: and ye shall find rest unto your souls.

For my yoke is easy, and my burden is light.

Matthew 11:28-30

How To Overcome Despair

We are troubled on every side, yet not distressed; we are perplexed, but not in despair;

Persecuted, but not forsaken; cast down, but not destroyed;

For which cause we faint not; but though our outward man perish, yet the inward man is renewed day by day.

For our light affliction, which is but for a moment, worketh for us a far more exceeding and eternal weight of glory;

While we look not at the things which are seen, but at the things which are not seen: for the things which are seen are temporal; but the things which are not seen are eternal.

II Corinthians 4:8-9, 16-18

Let your conversation be without covetousness; and be content with such things as ye have: for he hath said, I will never leave thee, nor forsake thee.

So that we may boldly say, The Lord is my helper, and I will not fear what man shall do unto me.

Hebrews 13:5-6

Come unto me, all ye that labour and are heavy laden, and I will give you rest.

Take my yoke upon you, and learn of me; for I am meek and lowly in heart; and ye shall find rest unto your souls.

For my yoke is easy, and my burden is light.

Matthew 11:28-30

For his anger endureth but a moment; in his favour is life: weeping may endure for a night, but joy cometh in the morning.

I cried to thee, O LORD; and unto the LORD I made supplication.

What profit is there in my blood, when I go down to the pit? Shall the dust praise thee? shall it declare thy truth?

Hear, O LORD, and have mercy upon me: LORD, be thou my helper.

Thou hast turned for me my mourning into dancing: thou hast put off my sackcloth, and girded me with gladness;

To the end that my glory may sing praise to thee, and not be silent. O LORD my God, I will give thanks unto thee for ever.

Psalm 30:5, 8-12

Finally, brethren, whatsoever things are true, whatsoever things are honest, whatsoever things are just, whatsoever things are pure, whatsoever things are lovely, whatsoever things are of good report; if there be any virtue, and if there be any praise, think on these things.

Philippians 4:8

For if ye turn again unto the LORD, your brethren and your children shall find compassion before them that lead them captive, so that they shall come again into this land: for the LORD your God is gracious and merciful, and will not turn away his face from you, if ye return unto him.

II Chronicles 30:9

He hath not dealt with us after our sins; nor rewarded us according to our iniquities.

For as the heaven is high above the earth, so great is his mercy toward them that fear him.

As far as the east is from the west, so far hath he removed our transgressions from us.

Psalm 103:10-12

Which hope we have as an anchor of the soul, both sure and stedfast, and which entereth into that within the veil;

Hebrews 6:19

And so, after he had patiently endured he obtained the promise.

Hebrews 6:15

And let us not be weary in well doing: for in due season we shall reap, if we faint not.

Galatians 6:9

THE spirit of the Lord GOD is upon me; because the LORD hath anointed me to preach good tidings unto the meek; he hath sent me to bind up the brokenhearted, to proclaim liberty to the captives, and the opening of the prison to them that are bound;

To proclaim the acceptable year of the LORD, and the day of vengeance of our God; to comfort all that mourn;

To appoint unto them that mourn in Zion, to give unto them beauty for ashes, the oil of joy for mourning, the garment of praise for the spirit of heaviness; that they might be called trees of righteousness, the planting of the LORD, that he might be glorified.

Isaiah 61:1-3

He giveth power to the faint; and to them that have no might he increaseth strength.

Even the youths shall faint and be weary, and the young men shall utterly fall:

But they that wait upon the LORD shall renew their strength; they shall mount up with wings as eagles; they shall run, and not be weary; and they shall walk, and not faint.

Isaiah 40:29-31

He healeth the broken in heart, and bindeth up their wounds.

Psalm 147:3

I know both how to be abased, and I know how to abound: every where and in all things I am instructed both to be full and to be hungry, both to abound and to suffer need.

I can do all things through Christ which strengtheneth me.

Philippians 4:12-13

And we have known and believed the love that God hath to us. God is love; and he that dwelleth in love dwelleth in God, and God in him.

I John 4:16

How To Maintain Hope

It is of the LORD's mercies that we are not consumed, because his compassions fail not.

They are new every morning: great is thy faithfulness.

The LORD is my portion, saith my soul; therefore will I hope in him.

Lamentations 3:22-24

THEREFORE being justified by faith, we have peace with God through our Lord Jesus Christ:

By whom also we have access by faith into this grace wherein we stand, and rejoice in hope of the glory of God.

And not only so, but we glory in tribulations also: knowing that tribulation worketh patience;

And patience, experience; and experience, hope:

And hope maketh not ashamed; because the love of God is shed abroad in our hearts by the Holy Ghost which is given unto us.

Romans 5:1-5

Now the God of hope fill you with all joy and peace in believing, that ye may abound in hope, through the power of the Holy Ghost.

Romans 15:13

But let us, who are of the day, be sober, putting on the breastplate of faith and love; and for an helmet, the hope of salvation.

For God hath not appointed us to wrath, but to obtain salvation by our Lord Jesus Christ.

I Thessalonians 5:8-9

Take therefore no thought for the morrow: for the morrow shall take thought for the things of itself. Sufficient unto the day is the evil thereof.

Matthew 6:34

Let your conversation be without covetousness; and be content with such things as ye have: for he hath said, I will never leave thee, nor forsake thee.

So that we may boldly say, The Lord is my helper, and I will not fear what man shall do unto me.

Hebrews 13:5-6

Behold, the eye of the LORD is upon them that fear him, upon them that hope in his mercy;

To deliver their soul from death, and to keep them alive in famine.

Our soul waiteth for the LORD: he is our help and our shield.

For our heart shall rejoice in him, because we have trusted in his holy name.

Let thy mercy, O LORD, be upon us, according as we hope in thee.

Psalm 33:18-22

Cast thy burden upon the LORD, and he shall sustain thee: he shall never suffer the righteous to be moved.

Psalm 55:22

My soul, wait thou only upon God; for my expectation is from him.

He only is my rock and my salvation: he is my defence; I shall not be moved.

In God is my salvation and my glory: the rock of my strength, and my refuge, is in God.

Psalm 62:5-7

I had fainted, unless I had believed to see the goodness of the LORD in the land of the living.

Wait on the LORD: be of good courage, and he shall strengthen thine heart: wait, I say, on the LORD.

Psalm 27:13-14

Thou art my hiding place and my shield: I hope in thy word.

Psalm 119:114

But they that wait upon the LORD shall renew their strength; they shall mount up with wings as eagles; they shall run, and not be weary; and they shall walk, and not faint.

Isaiah 40:31

Finally, brethren, whatsoever things are true, whatsoever things are honest, whatsoever things are just, whatsoever things are pure, whatsoever things are lovely, whatsoever things are of good report; if there be any virtue, and if there be any praise, think on these things.

I can do all things through Christ which strengtheneth me.

Philippians 4:8, 13

Or saith he it altogether for our sakes? For our sakes, no doubt, this is written: that he that ploweth should plow in hope; and that he that thresheth in hope should be partaker of his hope.

I Corinthians 9:10

And so, after he had patiently endured he obtained the promise.

That by two immutable things, in which it was impossible for God to lie, we might have a strong consolation, who have fled for refuge to lay hold upon the hope set before us:

Which hope we have as an anchor of the soul, both sure and stedfast, and which entereth into that within the veil;

Hebrews 6:15, 18-19

But if we hope for that we see not, then do we with patience wait for it.

What shall we then say to these things? If God be for us, who can be against us?

Nay, in all these things we are more than conquerors through him that loved us.

For I am persuaded, that neither death, nor life, nor angels, nor principalities, nor powers, nor things present, nor things to come,

Nor height, nor depth, nor any other creature, shall be able to separate us from the love of God, which is in Christ Jesus our Lord.

Romans 8:25, 31, 37-39

Be not a terror unto me: thou art my hope in the day of evil.

Jeremiah 17:17

How To Enter Into His Rest

Commit thy way unto the LORD; trust also in him; and he shall bring it to pass.

And he shall bring forth thy righteousness as the light, and thy judgment as the noonday.

Rest in the LORD, and wait patiently for him: fret not thyself because of him who prospereth in his way, because of the man who bringeth wicked devices to pass.

Psalm 37:5-7

Finally, brethren, whatsoever things are true, whatsoever things are honest, whatsoever things are just, whatsoever things are pure, whatsoever things are lovely, whatsoever things are of good report; if there be any virtue, and if there be any praise, think on these things.

Not that I speak in respect of want: for I have learned, in whatsoever state I am, therewith to be content.

I know both how to be abased, and I know how to abound: every where and in all things I am instructed both to be full and to be hungry, both to abound and to suffer need.

I can do all things through Christ which strengtheneth me.

But my God shall supply all your need according to his riches in glory by Christ Jesus.

Philippians 4:8, 11-13, 19

Come unto me, all ye that labour and are heavy laden, and I will give you rest.

Take my yoke upon you, and learn of me; for I am meek and lowly in heart: and ye shall find rest unto your souls.

For my yoke is easy, and my burden is light.

Matthew 11:28-30

There remaineth therefore a rest to the people of God.

Let us labour therefore to enter into that rest, lest any man fall after the same example of unbelief.

Seeing then that we have a great high priest, that is passed into the heavens, Jesus the Son of God, let us hold fast our profession.

Hebrews 4:9, 11, 14

For thus saith the Lord GOD, the Holy One of Israel; In returning and rest shall ye be saved; in quietness and in confidence shall be your strength: and ye would not.

And therefore will the LORD wait, that he may be gracious unto you, and therefore will he be exalted, that he may have mercy upon you: for the LORD is a God of judgment: blessed are all they that wait for him.

Isaiah 30:15, 18

The LORD is thy keeper: the LORD is thy shade upon thy right hand.

The sun shall not smite thee by day, nor the moon by night.

The LORD shall preserve thee from all evil: he shall preserve thy soul.

The LORD shall preserve thy going out and thy coming in from this time forth, and even for evermore.

Psalm 121:5-8

Cast thy burden upon the LORD, and he shall sustain thee: he shall never suffer the righteous to be moved.

Psalm 55:22

And he said, My presence shall go with thee, and I will give thee rest.

Exodus 33:14

And we know that all things work together for good to them that love God, to them who are the called according to his purpose.

Romans 8:28

Therefore being justified by faith, we have peace with God through our Lord Jesus Christ:

By whom also we have access by faith into this grace wherein we stand, and rejoice in hope of the glory of God.

Romans 5:1-2

For God is not the author of confusion, but of peace, as in all churches of the saints.

I Corinthians 14:33

The fear of man bringeth a snare: but whoso putteth his trust in the LORD shall be safe.

Proverbs 29:25

But seek ye first the kingdom of God, and his righteousness; and all these things shall be added unto you.

Take therefore no thought for the morrow: for the morrow shall take thought for the things of itself. Sufficient unto the day is the evil thereof.

Matthew 6:33, 34

Furthermore we have had fathers of our flesh which corrected us, and we gave them reverence: shall we not much rather be in subjection unto the Father of Spirits, and live?

Hebrews 12:9

Submit yourselves therefore to God. Resist the devil, and he will flee from you.

James 4:7

But the Lord is faithful, who shall stablish you, and keep you from evil.

II Thessalonians 3:3

How To Be Established In Trust

Blessed is the man that trusteth in the LORD, and whose hope the LORD is.

For he shall be as a tree planted by the waters, and that spreadeth out her roots by the river, and shall not see when heat cometh, but her leaf shall be green; and shall not be careful in the year of drought, neither shall cease from yielding fruit.

Jeremiah 17:7-8

And we know that all things work together for good to them that love God, to them who are the called according to his purpose.

Romans 8:28

I will say of the LORD, He is my refuge and my fortress: my God; in him will I trust.

Surely he shall deliver thee from the snare of the fowler, and from the noisome pestilence.

He shall cover thee with his feathers, and under his wings shalt thou trust: his truth shall be thy shield and buckler.

Psalm 91:2-4

Casting all your care upon him; for he careth for you.

I Peter 5:7

But the salvation of the righteous is of the LORD: he is their strength in the time of trouble.

And the LORD shall help them, and deliver them: he shall deliver them from the wicked, and save them, because they trust in him.

Psalm 37:39-40

He shall not be afraid of evil tidings: his heart is fixed, trusting in the LORD.

His heart is established, he shall not be afraid, until he see his desire upon his enemies.

Psalm 112:7-8

But we had the sentence of death in ourselves, that we should not trust in ourselves, but in God which raiseth the dead:

Who delivered us from so great a death, and doth deliver: in whom we trust that he will yet deliver us;

II Corinthians 1:9-10

Therefore will not we fear, though the earth be removed, and though the mountains be carried into the midst of the sea;

Psalm 46:2

Through God we shall do valiantly: for he it is that shall tread down our enemies.

Psalm 60:12

What time I am afraid, I will trust in thee.

In God I will praise his word, In God I have put my trust; I will not fear what flesh can do unto me.

In God have I put my trust: I will not be afraid what man can do unto me.

For thou hast delivered my soul from death: wilt not thou deliver my feet from falling, that I may walk before God in the light of the living?

Psalm 56:3-4, 11, 13

The LORD is on my side; I will not fear: what can man do unto me?

It is better to trust in the LORD than to put confidence in man.

Psalm 118:6, 8

He will not suffer thy foot to be moved: he that keepeth thee will not slumber.

Psalm 121:3

They that trust in the LORD shall be as mount Zion, which cannot be removed, but abideth for ever.

Do good, O LORD, unto those that be good, and to them that are upright in their hearts.

Psalm 125:1, 4

He that handleth a matter wisely shall find good: and whoso trusteth in the LORD, happy is he.

Proverbs 16:20

Every word of God is pure: he is a shield unto them that put their trust in him.

Proverbs 30:5

But thou, O LORD, art a shield for me; my glory, and the lifter up of mine head.

I cried unto the LORD with my voice, and he heard me out of his holy hill. Selah.

I laid me down and slept; I awaked; for the LORD sustained me.

I will not be afraid of ten thousands of people, that have set themselves against me round about.

Psalm 3:3-6

The LORD redeemeth the soul of his servants: and none of them that trust in him shall be desolate.

Psalm 34:22

Hold up my goings in thy paths, that my footsteps slip not.

I have called upon thee, for thou wilt hear me, O God: incline thine ear unto me, and hear my speech.

Shew thy marvellous lovingkindness, O thou that savest by thy right hand them which put their trust in thee from those that rise up against them.

Keep me as the apple of the eye, hide me under the shadow of thy wings,

Psalm 17:5-8

What To Do When You Are Facing Old Age

The righteous shall flourish like the palm tree: he shall grow like a cedar in Lebanon.

Those that be planted in the house of the LORD shall flourish in the courts of our God.

They shall still bring forth fruit in old age; they shall be fat and flourishing;

To shew that the LORD is upright: he is my rock, and there is no unrighteousness in him.

Psalm 92:12-15

Who satisfieth thy mouth with good things; so that thy youth is renewed like the eagle's.

Psalm 103:5

For by me thy days shall be multiplied, and the years of thy life shall be increased.

Proverbs 9:11

That the aged men be sober, grave, temperate, sound in faith, in charity, in patience.

The aged women likewise, that they be in behaviour as becometh holiness, not false accusers, not given to much wine, teachers of good things;

That they may teach the young women to be sober, to love their husbands, to love their children,

Titus 2:2-4

The days of our years are threescore years and ten; and if by reason of strength they be four-score years, yet is their strength labour and sorrow; for it is soon cut off, and we fly away.

So teach us to number our days, that we may apply our hearts unto wisdom.

O satisfy us early with thy mercy; that we may rejoice and be glad all our days.

Psalm 90:10, 12, 14

For none of us liveth to himself, and no man dieth to himself.

For whether we live, we live unto the Lord; and whether we die, we die unto the Lord: whether we live therefore, or die, we are the Lord's.

Romans 14:7-8

For I know that my redeemer liveth, and that he shall stand at the latter day upon the earth:

And though after my skin worms destroy this body, yet in my flesh shall I see God:

Whom I shall see for myself, and mine eyes shall behold, and not another; though my reins be consumed within me.

Job 19:25-27

Thou shalt guide me with thy counsel, and afterward receive me to glory.

Whom have I in heaven but thee? and there is none upon earth that I desire beside thee.

My flesh and my heart faileth: but God is the strength of my heart, and my portion for ever.

Psalm 73:24-26

For this God is our God for ever and ever: he will be our guide even unto death.

Psalm 48:14

Therefore remove sorrow from thy heart, and put away evil from thy flesh: for childhood and youth are vanity.

Ecclesiastes 11:10

But I trusted in thee, O LORD: I said, Thou art my God.

My times are in thy hand: deliver me from the hand of mine enemies, and from them that persecute me.

Psalm 31:14-15

For which cause we faint not; but though our outward man perish, yet the inward man is renewed day by day.

For our light affliction, which is but for a moment, worketh for us a far more exceeding and eternal weight of glory;

While we look not at the things which are seen, but at the things which are not seen: for the things which are seen are temporal; but the things which are not seen are eternal.

II Corinthians 4:16-18

For we know that if our earthly house of this tabernacle were dissolved, we have a building of God, an house not made with hands, eternal in the heavens.

II Corinthians 5:1

The fear of the LORD prolongeth days: but the years of the wicked shall be shortened.

Proverbs 10:27

Thou shalt come to thy grave in a full age, like as a shock of corn cometh in in his season.

Job 5:26

He will swallow up death in victory; and the Lord GOD will wipe away tears from off all faces; and the rebuke of his people shall he take away from off all the earth: for the LORD hath spoken it.

Isaiah 25:8

How To Have God's Divine Protection

HE that dwelleth in the secret place of the most High shall abide under the shadow of the Almighty.

I will say of the LORD, He is my refuge and my fortress: my God; in him will I trust.

Surely he shall deliver thee from the snare of the fowler, and from the noisome pestilence.

He shall cover thee with his feathers, and under his wings shalt thou trust: his truth shall be thy shield and buckler.

Thou shalt not be afraid for the terror by night; nor for the arrow that flieth by day;

Nor for the pestilence that walketh in darkenss; nor for the destruction that wasteth at noonday.

A thousand shall fall at thy side, and ten thousand at thy right hand; but it shall not come nigh thee.

Only with thine eyes shalt thou behold and see the reward of the wicked.

Because thou hast made the LORD, which is my refuge, even the most High, thy habitation;

There shall no evil befall thee, neither shall any plague come nigh thy dwelling.

For he shall give his angels charge over thee, to keep thee in all thy ways.

They shall bear thee up in their hands, lest thou dash thy foot against a stone.

Thou shalt tread upon the lion and adder: the young lion and the dragon shalt thou trample under feet.

Because he hath set his love upon me, therefore will I deliver him: I will set him on high, because he hath known my name.

He shall call upon me, and I will answer him: I will be with him in trouble; I will deliver him, and honour him.

With long life will I satisfy him, and shew him my salvation.

Psalm 91:1-16

THE LORD is my light and my salvation; whom shall I fear? the LORD is the strength of my life; of whom shall I be afraid?

For in the time of trouble he shall hide me in his pavilion: in the secret of his tabernacle shall he hide me; he shall set me up upon a rock.

Psalm 27:1, 5

When thou passest through the waters, I will be with thee; and through the rivers, they shall not overflow thee: when thou walkest through the fire, thou shalt not be burned; neither shall the flame kindle upon thee.

Isaiah 43:2

But let all those that put their trust in thee rejoice: let them ever shout for joy, because thou defendest them: let them also that love thy name be joyful in thee.

For thou, LORD, wilt bless the righteous; with favour wilt thou compass him as with a shield.

Psalm 5:11-12

And of Benjamin he said, The beloved of the LORD shall dwell in safety by him; and the LORD shall cover him all day long, and he shall dwell between his shoulders.

The eternal God is thy refuge, and underneath are the everlasting arms: and he shall thrust out the enemy from before thee; and shall say, Destroy them.

Deuteronomy 33:12, 27

Be careful for nothing; but in every thing by prayer and supplication with thanksgiving let your requests be made known unto God.

And the peace of God, which passeth all understanding, shall keep your hearts and minds through Christ Jesus.

Philippians 4:6-7

The angel of the LORD encampeth round about them that fear him, and delivereth them.

Psalm 34:7

The horse is prepared against the day of battle: but safety is of the LORD.

Proverbs 21:31

Are not two sparrows sold for a farthing? and one of them shall not fall on the ground without your Father.

But the very hairs of your head are all numbered.

Fear ye not therefore, ye are of more value than many sparrows.

Matthew 10:29-31

The fear of man bringeth a snare: but whoso putteth his trust in the LORD shall be safe.

Proverbs 29:25

Yea, though I walk through the valley of the shadow of death, I will fear no evil: for thou art with me; thy rod and thy staff they comfort me.

Psalm 23:4

So shall they fear the name of the LORD from the west, and his glory from the rising of the sun. When the enemy shall come in like a flood, the spirit of the LORD shall lift up a standard against him.

Isaiah 59:19

I will both lay me down in peace, and sleep; for thou, LORD, only makest me dwell in safety.

Psalm 4:8

He suffered no man to do them wrong: yea, he reproved kings for their sakes;

Saying, Touch not mine anointed, and do my prophets no harm.

Psalm 105:14-15

But whoso hearkeneth unto me shall dwell safely, and shall be quiet from fear of evil.

Proverbs 1:33

How To Find Contentment

Therefore take no thought, saying, What shall we eat? or, What shall we drink? or, Wherewithal shall we be clothed?

(For after all these things do the Gentiles seek:) for your heavenly Father knoweth that ye have need of all these things.

But seek ye first the kingdom of God, and his righteousness; and all these things shall be added unto you.

Take therefore no thought for the morrow: for the morrow shall take thought for the things of itself. Sufficient unto the day is the evil thereof.

Matthew 6:31-34

Thou wilt keep him in perfect peace, whose mind is stayed on thee:

Trust ye in the LORD for ever: for in the LORD JEHOVAH is everlasting strength:

Isaiah 26:3A-4

Let your conversation be without covetousness; and be content with such things as ye have: for he hath said, I will never leave thee, nor forsake thee.

So that we may boldly say, The Lord is my helper, and I will not fear what man shall do unto me.

Hebrews 13:5-6

Be careful for nothing; but in every thing by prayer and supplication with thanksgiving let your requests be made known unto God.

And the peace of God, which passeth all understanding, shall keep your hearts and minds through Christ Jesus.

Not that I speak in respect of want; for I have learned, in whatsoever state I am, therewith to be content.

I know both how to be abased, and I know how to abound: every where and in all things I am instructed both to be full and to be hungry, both to abound and to suffer need.

I can do all things through Christ which strengtheneth me.

Philippians 4:6, 7, 11-13

And we know that all things work together for good to them that love God, to them who are the called according to his purpose.

Romans 8:28

For the mountains shall depart, and the hills be removed; but my kindness shall not depart from thee; neither shall the covenant of my peace be removed, saith the LORD that hath mercy on thee.

And all thy children shall be taught of the LORD; and great shall be the peace of thy children.

No weapon that is formed against thee shall prosper; and every tonguc that shall rise against thee in judgment thou shalt condemn. This is the heritage of the servants of the LORD, and their righteousness is of me, saith the LORD.

Isaiah 54:10, 13, 17

THERE is therefore now no condemnation to them which are in Christ Jesus, who walk not after the flesh, but after the Spirit.

For the law of the Spirit of life in Christ Jesus hath made me free from the law of sin and death.

For they that are after the flesh do mind the things of the flesh; but they that are after the Spirit the things of the Spirit.

For to be carnally minded is death; but to be spiritually minded is life and peace.

Romans 8:1-2, 5-6

The Spirit itself beareth witness with our spirit, that we are the children of God:

And if children, then heirs; heirs of God, and joint-heirs with Christ; if so be that we suffer with him, that we may be also glorified together.

For I reckon that the sufferings of this present time are not worthy to be compared with the glory which shall be revealed in us.

Romans 8:16-18

He that dwelleth in the secret place of the most High shall abide under the shadow of the Almighty.

I will say of the LORD, he is my refuge and my fortress: my God; in him will I trust.

Psalm 91:1-2

The LORD upholdeth all that fall, and raiseth up all those that be bowed down.

Thc eyes of all wait upon thee; and thou givest them their meat in due season.

Thou openest thine hand, and satisifiest the desire of every living thing.

Psalm 145:14-16

But I keep under my body, and bring it into subjection: lest that by any means, when I have preached to others, I myself should be a castaway.

I Corinthians 9:27

But godliness with contentment is great gain.

For we brought nothing into this world, and it is certain we can carry nothing out.

And having food and raiment let us be therewith content.

I Timothy 6:6-8

But thou, O LORD, art a shield for me; my glory, and the lifter up of mine head.

I cried unto the LORD with my voice, and he heard me out of his holy hill. Selah.

I laid me down and slept; I awaked; for the LORD sustained me.

I will not be afraid of ten thousands of people, that have set themselves against me round about.

Psalm 3:3-6

For we which have believed do enter into rest, as he said, As I have sworn in my wrath, if they shall enter into my rest: although the works were finished from the foundation of the world.

Hebrews 4:3

And be found in him, not having mine own righteousness, which is of the law, but that which is through the faith of Christ, the righteousness which is of God by faith:

Philippians 3:9

THE LORD is my shepherd; I shall not want.

Psalm 23:1

And the LORD shall guide thee continually, and satisfy thy soul in drought, and make fat thy bones: and thou shalt be like a watered garden, and like a spring of water, whose waters fail not.

Isaiah 58:11

I WILL lift up mine eyes unto the hills, from whence cometh my help.

My help cometh from the LORD, which made heaven and earth.

He will not suffer thy foot to be moved: he that keepeth thee will not slumber.

The LORD is thy keeper: the LORD is thy shade upon thy right hand.

The LORD shall preserve thy going out and thy coming in from this time forth, and even for evermore.

Psalm 121:1-3, 5, 8

"...Shall not the Judge of all the earth do right?"

Genesis 18:25b

Not that we are sufficient of ourselves to think any thing as of ourselves; but our sufficiency is of God;

II Corinthians 3:5

Ministering In Christ...

What Is The Way To True Service?

And when he had called the people unto him with his disciples also, he said unto them, Whosoever will come after me, let him deny himself, and take up his cross, and follow me.

For whosoever will save his life shall lose it; but whosoever shall lose his life for my sake and the gospel's the same shall save it.

For what shall it profit a man, if he shall gain the whole world, and lose his own soul?

Or what shall a man give in exchange for his soul?

Mark 8:34-37

Abide in me, and I in you. As the branch cannot bear fruit of itself, except it abide in the vine; no more can ye, except ye abide in me.

I am the vine, ye are the branches: He that abideth in me, and I in him, the same bringeth forth much fruit: for without me ye can do nothing.

John 15:4-5

For we preach not ourselves, but Christ Jesus the Lord; and ourselves your servants for Jesus' sake.

For God, who commanded the light to shine out of darkness, hath shined in our hearts, to give the light of the knowledge of the glory of God in the face of Jesus Christ.

But we have this treasure in earthen vessels, that the excellency of the power may be of God, and not of us.

II Corinthians 4:5-7

And whatsoever ye do, do it heartily, as to the Lord, and not unto men;

Knowing that of the Lord ye shall receive the reward of the inheritance: for ye serve the Lord Christ.

But he that doeth wrong shall receive for the wrong which he hath done: and there is no respect of persons.

Colossians 3:23-25

Charge them that are rich in this world, that they be not high-minded, nor trust in uncertain riches, but in the living God, who giveth us richly all things to enjoy;

That they do good, that they be rich in good works, ready to distribute, willing to communicate;

Laying up in store for themselves a good foundation against the time to come, that they may lay hold on eternal life.

I Timothy 6:17-19

He that is faithful in that which is least is faithful also in much: and he that is unjust in the least is unjust also in much.

If therefore ye have not been faithful in the unrighteous mammon, who will commit to your trust the true riches?

And if ye have not been faithful in that which is another man's, who shall give you that which is your own?

No servant can serve two masters: for either he will hate the one, and love the other; or else he will hold to the one, and despise the other: Ye cannot serve God and mammon.

Luke 16:10-13

As every man hath received the gift, even so minister the same one to another, as good stewards of the manifold grace of God.

If any man speak, let him speak as the oracles of God; if any man minister, let him do it as of the ability which God giveth: that God in all things may be glorified through Jesus Christ, to whom be praise and dominion for ever and ever. Amen.

I Peter 4:10-11

Let every man abide in the same calling wherein he was called.

I Corinthians 7:20

John answered and said, A man can receive nothing, except it be given him from heaven.

John 3:27

But let every man prove his own work, and then shall he have rejoicing in himself alone, and not in another.

For every man shall bear his own burden.

Let him that is taught in the word communicate unto him that teacheth in all good things.

And let us not be weary in well doing: for in due season we shall reap, if we faint not.

Galatians 6:4-6, 9

Now he that planteth and he that watereth are one: and every man shall receive his own reward according to his own labour.

For we are labourers together with God: ye are God's husbandry, ye are God's building.

I Corinthians 3:8-9

For ye see your calling, brethren, how that not many wise men after the flesh, not many mighty, not many noble, are called:

But God hath chosen the foolish things of the world to confound the wise; and God hath chosen the weak things of the world to confound the things which are mighty;

And base things of the world, and things which are despised, hath God chosen, yea, and things which are not, to bring to nought things that are:

That no flesh should glory in his presence.

I Corinthians 1:26-29

But a certain Samaritan, as he journeyed, came where he was: and when he saw him, he had compassion on him,

And went to him, and bound up his wounds, pouring in oil and wine, and set him on his own beast, and brought him to an inn, and took care of him.

Luke 10:33-34

In the morning sow thy seed, and in the evening withhold not thine hand: for thou knowest not whether shall prosper, either this or that, or whether they both shall be alike good.

Ecclesiastes 11:6

And another also said, Lord, I will follow thee; but let me first go bid them farewell, which are at home at my house.

And Jesus said unto him, No man, having put his hand to the plough, and looking back, is fit for the kingdom of God.

Luke 9:61-62

Doth he thank that servant because he did the things that were commanded him? I trow not.

So likewise ye, when ye shall have done all those things which are commanded you, say, We are unprofitable servants: we have done that which was our duty to do.

Luke 17:9-10

And the people asked him, saying, What shall we do then?

He answereth and saith unto them, He that hath two coats, let him impart to him that hath none; and he that hath meat, let him do likewise.

Luke 3:10-11

By this shall all men know that ye are my disciples, if ye have love one to another.

John 13:35

That ye may be blameless and harmless, the sons of God, without rebuke, in the midst of a crooked and perverse nation, among whom ye shine as lights in the world;

Holding forth the word of life; that I may rejoice in the day of Christ, that I have not run in vain, neither laboured in vain.

Philippians 2:15-16

Ye have not chosen me, but I have chosen you, and ordained you, that ye should go and bring forth fruit, and that your fruit should remain: that whatsoever ye shall ask of the Father in my name, he may give it you.

These things I command you, that ye love one another.

John 15:16-17

And whosoever doth not bear his cross, and come after me, cannot be my disciple.

For which of you, intending to build a tower, sitteth not down first, and counteth the cost, whether he have sufficient to finish it?

Lest haply, after he hath laid the foundation, and is not able to finish it, all that behold it begin to mock him.

Saying, This man began to build, and was not able to finish.

So likewise, whosoever he be of you that forsaketh not all that he hath, he cannot be my disciple.

Luke 14:27-30, 33

Faithful is he that calleth you, who also will do it.

I Thessalonians 5:24

How To Have An Effective Prayer Life

Be careful for nothing; but in every thing by prayer and supplication with thanksgiving let your request be made known unto God.

And the peace of God, which passeth all understanding, shall keep your hearts and minds through Christ Jesus.

Philippians 4:6-7

Verily I say unto you, Whatsoever ye shall bind on earth shall be bound in heaven: and whatsoever ye shall loose on earth shall be loosed in heaven.

Again I say unto you, That if two of you shall agree on earth as touching any thing that they shall ask, it shall be done for them of my Father which is in heaven.

Matthew 18:18-19

Let us therefore come boldly unto the throne of grace, that we may obtain mercy, and find grace to help in time of need:

Hebrews 4:16

But without faith it is impossible to please him; for he that cometh to God must believe that he is, and that he is a rewarder of them that diligently seek him.

Hebrews 11:6

Confess your faults one to another, and pray one for another, that ye may be healed. The effectual fervent prayer of a righteous man availeth much.

Elias was a man subject to like passions as we are, and he prayed earnestly that it might not rain: and it rained not on the earth by the space of three years and six months.

And he prayed again, and the heaven gave rain, and the earth brought forth her fruit.

James 5:16-18

Wherefore take unto you the whole armour of God, that ye may be able to withstand in the evil day, and having done all, to stand.

Stand therefore, having your loins girt about with truth, and having on the breastplate of righteousness;

And your feet shod with the preparation of the gospel of peace;

Above all, taking the shield of faith, wherewith ye shall be able to quench all the fiery darts of the wicked.

And take the helmet of salvation, and the sword of the Spirit, which is the word of God:

Praying always with all prayer and supplication in the Spirit, and watching thereunto with all perseverance and supplication for all saints;

Ephesians 6:13-18

And I say unto you, Ask, and it shall be given you; seek, and ye shall find; knock, and it shall be opened unto you.

Luke 11:9

And when thou prayest, thou shalt not be as the hypocrites are: for they love to pray standing in the synagogues and in the corners of the streets, that they may be seen of men. Verily I say unto you, They have their reward.

But thou, when thou prayest, enter into thy closet, and when thou hast shut thy door, pray to the Father which is in secret; and thy Father which seeth in secret shall reward thee openly.

Matthew 6:5-6

And he spake a parable unto them to this end, that men ought always to pray, and not to faint;

Luke 18:1

For the eyes of the Lord are over the righteous, and his ears are open unto their prayers: but the face of the Lord is against them that do evil.

I Peter 3:12

Evening, and morning, and at noon, will I pray, and cry aloud: and he shall hear my voice.

Psalm 55:17

Let us come before his presence with thanksgiving, and make a joyful noise unto him with psalms.

Psalm 95:2

I CRIED unto the Lord with my voice; with my voice unto the LORD did I make my supplication.

I poured out my complaint before him; I shewed before him my trouble.

Psalm 142:1-2

And this is the confidence that we have in him, that, if we ask any thing according to his will, he heareth us:

And if we know that he hear us, whatsoever we ask, we know that we have the petitions that we desired of him.

I John 5:14-15

Thou shalt make thy prayer unto him, and he shall hear thee, and thou shalt pay thy vows.

Thou shalt also decree a thing, and it shall be established unto thee: and the light shall shine upon thy ways.

Job 22:27-28

Likewise the Spirit also helpeth our infirmities: for we know not what we should pray for as we ought: but the Spirit itself maketh intercession for us with groanings which cannot be uttered.

Romans 8:26

My voice shalt thou hear in the morning, O LORD; in the morning will I direct my prayer unto thee, and will look up.

Psalm 5:3

But know that the LORD hath set apart him that is godly for himself: the LORD will hear when I call unto him.

Psalm 4:3

Give ear, O LORD, unto my prayer; and attend to the voice of my supplications.

In the day of my trouble I will call upon thee: for thou wilt answer me.

Psalm 86:6-7

But let him ask in faith, nothing wavering. For he that wavereth is like a wave of the sea driven with the wind and tossed.

James 1:6

Thou calledst in trouble, and I delivered thee; I answered thee in the secret place of thunder: I proved thee at the waters of Meribah. Selah.

Psalm 81:7

Rejoicing in hope; patient in tribulation; continuing instant in prayer;

Romans 12:12

And in the morning, rising up a great while before day, he went out, and departed into a solitary place, and there prayed.

Mark 1:35

And it came to pass in those days, that he went out into a mountain to pray, and continued all night in prayer to God.

Luke 6:12

LORD, I cry unto thee: make haste unto me; give ear unto my voice, when I cry unto thee.

Let my prayer be set forth before thee as incense; and the lifting up of my hands as the evening sacrifice.

Psalm 141:1-2

So shall my word be that goeth forth out of my mouth: it shall not return unto me void, but it shall accomplish that which I please, and it shall prosper in the thing whereto I sent it.

Isaiah 55:11

How To Be An Effective Witness

Ye are the light of the world, A city that is set on an hill cannot be hid.

Neither do men light a candle, and put it under a bushel, but on a candelstick; and it giveth light unto all that are in the house.

Let your light so shine before men, that they may see your good works, and glorify your Father which is in heaven.

Matthew 5:14-16

No man, when he hath lighted a candle, putteth it in a secret place, neither under a bushel, but on a candlestick, that they which come in may see the light.

Luke 11:33

Finally, be ye all of one mind, having compassion one of another, love as brethren, be pitiful, be courteous:

Not rendering evil for evil, or railing for railing: but contrariwise blessing; knowing that ye are thereunto called, that ye should inherit a blessing.

For he that will love life, and see good days, let him refrain his tongue from evil, and his lips that they speak no guile:

Let him eschew evil, and do good; let him seek peace, and ensue it.

But sanctify the Lord God in your hearts: and be ready always to give an answer to every man that asketh you a reason of the hope that is in you with meekness and fear:

I Peter 3:8-11, 15

Also I say unto you, Whosoever shall confess me before men, him shall the Son of man also confess before the angels of God:

But he that denieth me before men shall be denied before the angels of God.

Luke 12:8-9

Praying always with all prayer and supplication in the Spirit, and watching thereunto with all perseverance and supplication for all saints;

And for me, that utterance may be given unto me, that I may open my mouth boldly, to make known the mystery of the gospel,

For which I am an ambassador in bonds: that therein I may speak boldly, as I ought to speak.

Ephesians 6:18-20

Study to shew thyself approved unto God, a workman that needeth not to be ashamed, rightly dividing the word of truth.

But shun profane and vain babblings: for they will increase unto more ungodliness.

But foolish and unlearned questions avoid, knowing that they do gender strifes.

And the servant of the Lord must not strive; but be gentle unto all men, apt to teach, patient,

In meekness instructing those that oppose themselves; if God peradventure will give them repentance to the acknowledging of the truth;

II Timothy 2:15-16, 23-25

A good man out of the good treasure of his heart bringeth forth that which is good; and an evil man out of the evil treasure of his heart bringeth forth that which is evil: for of the abundance of the heart his mouth speaketh.

Luke 6:45

Settle it therefore in your hearts, not to meditate before what ye shall answer:

For I will give you a mouth and wisdom, which all your adversaries shall not be able to gainsay nor resist.

Luke 21:14-15

By this shall all men know that ye are my disciples, if ye have love one to another.

John 13:35

What man of you, having an hundred sheep, if he lose one of them, doth not leave the ninety and nine in the wilderness, and go after that which is lost, until he find it?

And when he hath found it, he layeth it on his shoulders, rejoicing.

And when he cometh home, he calleth together his friends and neighbours, saying unto them, Rejoice with me; for I have found my sheep which was lost.

I say unto you, that likewise joy shall be in heaven over one sinner that repenteth, more than over ninety and nine just persons, which need no repentance.

Luke 15:4-7

The fruit of the righteous is a tree of life; and he that winneth souls is wise.

Proverbs 11:30

Be not thou therefore ashamed of the testimony of our Lord, nor of me his prisoner: but be thou partaker of the afflictions of the gospel according to the power of God;

Who hath saved us, and called us with an holy calling, not according to our works, but according to his own purpose and grace, which was given us in Christ Jesus before the world began.

But is now made manifest by the appearing of our Saviour Jesus Christ, who hath abolished death, and hath brought life and immortality to light through the gospel:

II Timothy 1:8-10

I will sing unto the LORD as long as I live: I will sing praise to my God while I have my being.

Psalm 104:33

For God is my witness, whom I serve with my spirit in the gospel of his Son, that without ceasing I make mention of you always in my prayers;

For I am not ashamed of the gospel of Christ: for it is the power of God unto salvation to every one that believeth; to the Jew first, and also to the Greek.

For therein is the righteousness of God revealed from faith to faith: as it is written, The just shall live by faith.

Romans 1:9, 16-17

Brethren, if any of you do err from the truth, and one convert him;

Let him know, that he which converteth the sinner from the error of his way, shall save a soul from death, and shall hide a multitude of sins.

James 5:19-20

But ye shall receive power, after that the Holy Ghost is come upon you: and ye shall be witnesses unto me both in Jerusalem, and in all Judaea, and in Samaria, and unto the uttermost part of the earth.

Acts 1:8

And he said unto them, Go ye into all the world, and preach the gospel to every creature.

Mark 16:15

And he said to them all, If any man will come after me, let him deny himself, and take up his cross daily, and follow me.

For whosoever will save his life shall lose it: but whosoever will lose his life for my sake, the same shall save it.

For what is a man advantaged, if he gain the whole world, and lose himself, or be cast away?

For whosoever shall be ashamed of me and of my words, of him shall the Son of man be ashamed, when he shall come in his own glory, and in his Father's, and of the holy angels.

Luke 9:23-26

Preach the word; be instant in season, out of season; reprove, rebuke, exhort with all longsuffering and doctrine.

II Timothy 4:2

Howbeit Jesus suffered him not, but saith unto him, Go home to thy friends, and tell them how great things the Lord hath done for thee, and hath had compassion on thee.

That I may publish with the voice of thanksgiving, and tell of all thy wondrous works.

Psalm 26:7

Let the words of my mouth, and the meditation of my heart, be acceptable in thy sight, O LORD, my strength, and my redeemer.

Psalm 19:14

How To Handle Condemnation

Blessed are ye, when men shall hate you, and when they shall separate you from their company, and shall reproach you, and cast out your name as evil, for the Son of man's sake.

Rejoice ye in that day, and leap for joy: for, behold, your reward is great in heaven: for in the like manner did their fathers unto the prophets.

Luke 6:22-23

If the world hate you, ye know that it hated me before it hated you.

If ye were of the world, the world would love his own: but because ye are not of the world, but I have chosen you out of the world, therefore the world hateth you.

Remember the word that I said unto you, The servant is not greater than his lord. If they have persecuted me, they will also persecute you; if they have kept my saying, they will keep yours also.

But all these things will they do unto you for my name's sake, because they know not him that sent me.

John 15:18-21

But and if ye suffer for righteousness' sake, happy are ye: and be not afraid of their terror, neither be troubled;

But sanctify the Lord God in your hearts: and be ready always to give an answer to every man that asketh you a reason of the hope that is in you with meekness and fear:

Having a good conscience; that, whereas they speak evil of you, as of evil-doers, they may be ashamed that falsely accuse your good conversation in Christ.

I Peter 3:14-16

If ye be reproached for the name of Christ, happy are ye; for the spirit of glory and of God resteth upon you: on their part he is evil spoken of, but on your part he is glorified.

Yet if any man suffer as a Christian, let him not be ashamed; but let him glorify God on this behalf.

I Peter 4:14, 16

Therefore being justified by faith, we have peace with God through our Lord Jesus Christ:

By whom also we have access by faith into this grace wherein we stand, and rejoice in hope of the glory of God.

Romans 5:1-2

Judge not, that ye be not judged.

For with what judgment ye judge, ye shall be judged: and with what measure ye mete, it shall be measured to you again.

And why beholdest thou the mote that is in thy brother's eye, but considerest not the beam that is in thine own eye?

Or how wilt thou say to thy brother, Let me pull out the mote out of thine eye; and, behold, a beam is in thine own eye?

Thou hypocrite, first cast out the beam out of thine own eye; and then shalt thou see clearly to cast out the mote out of thy brother's eye.

Give not that which is holy unto the dogs, neither cast ye your pearls before swine, lest they trample them under their feet, and turn again and rend you.

Matthew 7:1-6

But the LORD is my defense; and my God is the rock of my refuge.

And he shall bring upon them their own iniquity, and shall cut them off in their own wickedness; yea, the LORD our God shall cut them off.

Psalm 94:22-23

Mine eyes shall be upon the faithful of the land, that they may dwell with me: he that walketh in a perfect way, he shall serve me.

He that worketh deceit shall not dwell within my house: he that telleth lies shall not tarry in my sight.

Psalm 101:6-7

Say not thou, I will recompense evil; but wait on the LORD, and he shall save thee.

Proverbs 20:22

By faith Moses, when he was come to years, refused to be called the son of Pharaoh's daughter;

Choosing rather to suffer affliction with the people of God, than to enjoy the pleasures of sin for a season;

Esteeming the reproach of Christ greater riches than the treasures in Egypt: for he had respect unto the recompense of the reward.

Hebrews 11:24-26

Be not thou therefore ashamed of the testimony of our Lord, nor of me his prisoner: but be thou partaker of the afflictions of the gospel according to the power of God;

Who hath saved us, and called us with an holy calling, not according to our works, but according to his own purpose and grace which was given us in Christ Jesus before the world began,

II Timothy 1:8-9

Persecutions, afflictions, which came unto me at Antioch, at Iconium, at Lystra; what persecutions I endured: but out of them all the Lord delivered me.

Yea, and all that will live godly in Christ Jesus shall suffer persecution.

II Timothy 3:11-12

As it is written, There is none righteous, no, not one:

There is none that understandeth, there is none that seeketh after God.

They are all gone out of the way, they are together become unprofitable; there is none that doeth good, no, not one.

Romans 3:10-12

Cast out the scorner, and contention shall go out; yea, strife and reproach shall cease.

Proverbs 22:10

For this is thankworthy, if a man for conscience toward God endure grief, suffering wrongfully.

For what glory is it, if, when ye be buffeted for your faults, ye shall take it patiently? but if, when ye do well, and suffer for it, ye take it patiently, this is acceptable with God.

For even hereunto were ye called: because Christ also suffered for us, leaving us an example, that ye should follow his steps:

Who did no sin, neither was guile found in his mouth:

Who, when he was reviled, reviled not again; when he suffered, he threatened not; but committed himself to him that judgeth righteously:

Who his own self bare our sins in his own body on the tree, that we, being dead to sins, should live unto righteousness: by whose stripes ye were healed.

I Peter 2:19-24

Behold, all they that were incensed against thee shall be ashamed and confounded: they shall be as nothing; and they that strive with thee shall perish.

Thou shalt seek them, and shalt not find them, even them that contended with thee: they that war against thee shall be as nothing, and as a thing of nought.

For I the LORD thy God will hold thy right hand, saying unto thee, Fear not; I will help thee.

Isaiah 41:11-13

What Is The Leading Of The Lord?

And the LORD shall guide thee continually, and satisfy thy soul in drought, and make fat thy bones: and thou shalt be like a watered garden, and like a spring of water, whose waters fail not.

Isaiah 58:11

I say unto you, that likewise joy shall be in heaven over one sinner that repenteth, more than over ninety and nine just persons, which need no repentance.

Luke 15:7

For my thoughts are not your thoughts, neither are your ways my ways, saith the LORD.

For as the heavens are higher than the earth, so are my ways higher than your ways, and my thoughts than your thoughts.

Isaiah 55:8-9

BELOVED, believe not every spirit, but try the spirits whether they are of God: because many false prophets are gone out into the world.

I John 4:1

The Lord is not slack concerning his promise as some men count slackness; but is long-suffering to us-ward, not willing that any should perish, but that all should come to repentance.

II Peter 3:9

For the Son of man is come to save that which was lost.

Matthew 18:11

The spirit of man is the candle of the LORD, searching all the inward parts of the belly.

Proverbs 20:27

He found him in a desert land, and in the waste howling wilderness; he led him about, he instructed him, he kept him as the apple of his eye.

As an eagle stirreth up her nest, fluttereth over her young, spreadeth abroad her wings, taketh them, beareth them on her wings:

So the LORD alone did lead him, and there was no strange god with him.

Deuteronomy 32:10-12

So he fed them according to the integrity of his heart; and guided them by the skilfulness of his hands.

Psalm 78:72

For ye shall not go out with haste, nor go by flight: for the LORD will go before you; and the God of Israel will be your reward.

Isaiah 52:12

Shall a trumpet be blown in the city, and the people not be afraid? shall there be evil in a city, and the LORD hath not done it?

Surely the Lord GOD will do nothing, but he revealeth his secret unto his servants the prophets.

The lion hath roared, who will not fear? the Lord GOD hath spoken, who can but prophesy?

Amos 3:6-8

And by a prophet the LORD brought Israel out of Egypt, and by a prophet was he preserved.

Hosea 12:13

For there are three that bear record in heaven, the Father, the Word, and the Holy Ghost: and these three are one.

I John 5:7

And he said, Go forth, and stand upon the mount before the LORD. And behold, the LORD passed by, and a great and strong wind rent the mountains, and brake in pieces the rocks before the LORD; but the LORD was not in the wind: and after the wind an earthquake; but the LORD was not in the earthquake:

And after the earthquake a fire; but the LORD was not in the fire: and after the fire a still small voice.

I Kings 19:11-12

A man's heart deviseth his way: but the LORD directeth his steps.

The lot is cast into the lap; but the whole disposing thereof is of the LORD.

Proverbs 16:9, 33

For God hath not given us the spirit of fear; but of power, and of love, and of a sound mind.

II Timothy 1:7

How To Wait On God

Rest in the LORD, and wait patiently for him: fret not thyself because of him who prospereth in his way, because of the man who bringeth wicked devices to pass.

Cease from anger, and forsake wrath: fret not thyself in any wise to do evil.

For evildoers shall be cut off: but those that wait upon the LORD, they shall inherit the earth.

Psalm 37:7-9

I WAITED patiently for the LORD; and he inclined unto me, and heard my cry.

He brought me up also out of an horrible pit, out of the miry clay, and set my feet upon a rock, and established my goings.

And he hath put a new song in my mouth, even praise unto our God: many shall see it, and fear, and shall trust in the LORD.

Psalm 40:1-3

And therefore will the LORD wait, that he may be gracious unto you, and therefore will he be exalted, that he may have mercy upon you: for the LORD is a God of judgment: blessed are all they that wait for him.

Isaiah 30:18

Yea, let none that wait on thee be ashamed: let them be ashamed which transgress without cause.

Shew my thy ways, O LORD; teach me thy paths.

Lead me in thy truth, and teach me: for thou art the God of my salvation; on thee do I wait all the day.

Let integrity and uprightness preserve me; for I wait on thee.

Psalm 25:3-5, 21

Wait on the LORD: be of good courage, and he shall strengthen thine heart: wait, I say, on the LORD.

Psalm 27:14

But they that wait upon the LORD shall renew their strength; they shall mount up with wings as eagles; they shall run, and not be weary; and they shall walk, and not faint.

Isaiah 40:31

The LORD is good unto them that wait for him, to the soul that seeketh him.

It is good that a man should both hope and quietly wait for the salvation of the LORD.

Lamentations 3:25-26

Therefore I will look unto the LORD; I will wait for the God of my salvation: my God will hear me.

Micah 7:7

And ye yourselves like unto men that wait for their lord, when he will return from the wedding; that when he cometh and knocketh, they may open unto him immediately.

Luke 12:36

For they themselves shew of us what manner of entering in we had unto you, and how ye turned to God from idols to serve the living and true God;

And to wait for his Son from heaven, whom he raised from the dead, even Jesus, which delivered us from the wrath to come.

I Thessalonians 1:9-10

Therefore turn thou to thy God: for my expectation is from him.

He only is my rock and my salvation: he is my defence; I shall not be moved.

Psalm 62:5-6

I have waited for thy salvation, O LORD.

Genesis 49:18

The LORD upholdeth all that fall, and raiseth up all those that be bowed down.

The eyes of all wait upon thee; and thou givest them their meat in due season.

Psalm 145:14-15

And now, Lord, what wait I for? my hope is in thee.

Deliver me from all my transgressions: make me not the reproach of the foolish.

Psalm 39:7-8

They soon forgot his works; they waited not for his counsel:

Psalm 106:13

I wait for the LORD, my soul doth wait, and in his word do I hope.

My Soul waiteth for the Lord more than they that watch for the morning: I say, more than they that watch for the morning.

Psalm 130:5-6

And it shall be said in that day, Lo, this is our God; we have waited for him, and he will save us: this is the LORD; we have waited for him, we will be glad and rejoice in his salvation.

Isaiah 25:9

And kings shall be thy nursing fathers, and their queens thy nursing mothers: they shall bow down to thee with their face toward the earth, and lick up the dust of thy feet; and thou shalt know that I am the LORD: for they shall not be ashamed that wait for me.

Isaiah 49:23

For since the beginning of the world men have not heard, nor perceived by the ear, neither hath the eye seen, O God, beside thee, what he hath prepared for him that waiteth for him.

Isaiah 64:4

For the Egyptians shall help in vain, and to no purpose: therefore have I cried concerning this, Their strength is to sit still.

Isaiah 30:7

Let us hold fast the profession of our faith without wavering; (for he is faithful that promised;)

Hebrews 10:23

Therefore turn thou to thy God: keep mercy and judgment, and wait on thy God continually.

Hosea 12:6

What Is The Importance Of Obedience?

That all the people of the earth may know that the LORD is God, and that there is none else.

Let your heart therefore be perfect with the LORD our God, to walk in his statutes, and to keep his commandments, as at this day.

I Kings 8:60-61

But be ye doers of the word, and not hearers only, deceiving your own selves.

James 1:22

Now therefore, if ye will obey my voice indeed, and keep my covenant, then ye shall be a peculiar treasure unto me above all people: for all the earth is mine:

Exodus 19:5

Be not deceived; God is not mocked: for whatsoever a man soweth, that shall he also reap.

For he that soweth to his flesh shall of the flesh reap corruption; but he that soweth to the Spirit shall of the Spirit reap life everlasting.

Galatians 6:7-8

If ye love me, keep my commandments.

John 14:15

Whosoever cometh to me, and heareth my sayings, and doeth them, I will shew you to whom he is like:

He is like a man which built an house, and digged deep, and laid the foundation on a rock: and when the flood arose, the stream beat vehemently upon that house, and could not shake it: for it was founded upon a rock.

But he that heareth, and doeth not, is like a man that without a foundation built an house upon the earth; against which the stream did beat vehemently, and immediately it fell; and the ruin of that house was great.

Luke 6:47-49

Seest thou how faith wrought with his works, and by works was faith made perfect?

And the scripture was fulfilled which saith, Abraham believed God, and it was imputed unto him for righteousness: and he was called the Friend of God.

James 2:22-23

Then Peter and the other apostles answered and said, We ought to obey God rather than men.

Acts 5:29

For if there be first a willing mind, it is accepted according to that a man hath, and not according to that he hath not.

And not that only, but who was also chosen of the churches to travel with us with this grace, which is administered by us to the glory of the same Lord, and declaration of your ready mind:

II Corinthians 8:12, 19

But Jesus called them unto him, and said, Suffer little children to come unto me, and forbid them not: for of such is the kingdom of God.

Verily I say unto you, Whosoever shall not receive the kingdom of God as a little child shall in no wise enter therein.

Luke 18:16-17

But I keep under my body, and bring it into subjection: lest that by any means, when I have preached to others, I myself should be a castaway.

I Corinthians 9:27

Casting down imaginations, and every high thing that exalteth itself against the knowledge of God, and bringing into captivity every thought to the obedience of Christ;

II Corinthians 10:5

Furthermore we have had fathers of our flesh which corrected us, and we gave them reverence: shall we not much rather be in subjection unto the Father of spirits, and live?

For they verily for a few days chastened us after their own pleasure; but he for our profit, that we might be partakers of his holiness.

Hebrews 12:9-10

He that hath no rule over his own spirit is like a city that is broken down, and without walls.

Proverbs 25:28

He that is faithful in that which is least is faithful also in much: and he that is unjust in the least is unjust also in much.

Luke 16:10

But we see Jesus, who was made a little lower than the angels for the suffering of death, crowned with glory and honour; that he by the grace of God should taste death for every man.

For it became him, for whom are all things, and by whom are all things, in bringing many sons unto glory, to make the captain of their salvation perfect through sufferings.

Hebrews 2:9-10

Behold, thou desirest truth in the inward parts: and in the hidden part thou shalt make me to know wisdom.

Psalm 51:6

And when he had called the people unto him with his disciples also, he said unto them, Whosoever will come after me, let him deny himself, and take up his cross, and follow me.

For whosoever will save his life shall lose it; but whosoever shall lose his life for my sake and the gospel's the same shall save it.

For what shall it profit a man, if he shall gain the whole world, and lose his own soul?

Or what shall a man give in exchange for his soul?

Mark 8:34-37

And the world passeth away, and the lust thereof: but he that doeth the will of God abideth for ever.

I John 2:17

And rend your heart, and not your garments, and turn unto the LORD your God: for he is gracious and merciful, slow to anger, and of great kindness, and repenteth him of the evil.

Joel 2:13

If a man abide not in me, he is cast forth as a branch, and is withered; and men gather them, and cast them into the fire, and they are burned.

If ye abide in me, and my words abide in you, ye shall ask what ye will, and it shall be done unto you.

If ye keep my commandments, ye shall abide in my love; even as I have kept my Father's commandments, and abide in his love.

John 15:6-7, 10

If ye forsake the LORD, and serve strange gods, then he will turn and do you hurt, and consume you, after that he hath done you good.

Joshua 24:20

And the LORD was with Jehoshaphat, because he walked in the first ways of his father David, and sought not unto Ba-alim;

But sought to the LORD God of his father, and walked in his commandments, and not after the doings of Israel.

II Chronicles 17:3-4

Now the just shall live by faith: but if any man draw back, my soul shall have no pleasure in him.

Hebrews 10:38

And Samuel said, Hath the LORD as great delight in burnt offerings and sacrifices, as in obeying the voice of the LORD Behold, to obey is better than sacrifices, and to hearken than the fat of rams.

I Samuel 15:22

If ye be willing and obedient, ye shall eat the good of the land:

But if ye refuse and rebel, ye shall be devoured with the sword: for the mouth of the LORD hath spoken it.

Isaiah 1:19-20

How To Give To God's Work

Lay not up for yourselves treasures upon earth, where moth and rust doth corrupt, and where thieves break through and steal:

But lay up for yourselves treasures in heaven, where neither moth nor rust doth corrupt, and where thieves do not break through nor steal:

For where your treasure is, there will your heart be also.

Matthew 6:19-21

And Jesus sat over against the treasury, and beheld how the people cast money into the treasury: and many that were rich cast in much.

And there came a certain poor widow, and she threw in two mites, which make a farthing.

And he called unto him his disciples, and saith unto them, Verily I say unto you, That this poor widow hath cast more in than all they which have cast into the treasury.

For all they did cast in of their abundance; but she of her want did cast in all that she had, even all her living.

Mark 12:41-44

But this I say, He which soweth sparingly shall reap also sparingly; and he which soweth bountifully shall reap also bountifully.

Every man according as he purposeth in his heart, so let him give; not grudgingly, or of necessity: for God loveth a cheerful giver.

II Corinthians 9:6-7

When thou vowest a vow unto God, defer not to pay it; for he hath no pleasure in fools: pay that which thou hast vowed.

Better is it that thou shouldest not vow, than that thou shouldest vow, and not pay.

Suffer not thy mouth to cause thy flesh to sin; neither say thou before the angel, that it was an error: wherefore should God be angry at thy voice, and destroy the work of thine hands?

Ecclesiastes 5:4-6

Give unto the LORD the glory due unto his name: bring an offering, and come before him: worship the LORD in the beauty of holiness.

I Chronicles 16:29

Therefore when thou doest thine alms, do not sound a trumpet before thee, as the hypocrites do in the synagogues and in the streets, that they may have glory of men. Verily I say unto you, They have their reward.

But when thou doest alms, let not thy left hand know what thy right hand doeth:

That thine alms may be in secret: and thy Father which seeth in secret himself shall reward thee openly.

Matthew 6:2-4

Again, the kingdom of heaven is like unto treasure hid in a field; the which when a man hath found, he hideth, and for joy thereof goeth and selleth all that he hath, and buyeth that field.

Again, the kingdom of heaven is like unto a merchant man, seeking goodly pearls:

Who, when he had found one pearl of great price, went and sold all that he had, and bought it.

Matthew 13:44-46

Upon the first day of the week let every one of you lay by him in store, as God hath prospered him, that there be no gatherings when I come.

I Corinthians 16:2

And Elijah said unto her, Fear not; go and do as thou hast said: but make me thereof a little cake first, and bring it unto me, and after make for thee and for thy son.

For thus saith the LORD God of Israel, The barrel of meal shall not waste, neither shall the cruse of oil fail, until the day that the LORD sendeth rain upon the earth.

I Kings 17:13-14

Then the people rejoiced, for that they offered willingly, because with perfect heart they offered willingly to the LORD: and David the king also rejoiced with great joy.

I Chronicles 29:9

Give unto the LORD the glory due unto his name: bring an offering, and come into his courts.

Psalm 96:8

There is that scattereth, and yet increaseth; and there is that withholdeth more than is meet, but it tendeth to poverty.

The liberal soul shall be made fat: and he that watereth shall be watered also himself.

Proverbs 11:24-25

He that hath a bountiful eye shall be blessed; for he giveth of his bread to the poor.

Proverbs 22:9

The righteous considereth the cause of the poor: but the wicked regardeth not to know it.

Proverbs 29:7

Cast thy bread upon the waters: for thou shalt find it after many days.

Ecclesiastes 11:1

Take ye from among you an offering unto the LORD: whosoever is of a willing heart, let him bring it, an offering of the LORD; gold, and silver, and brass,

Exodus 35:5

And rend your heart, and not your garments, and turn unto the LORD your God: for he is gracious and merciful, slow to anger, and of great kindness, and repenteth him of the evil.

Who knoweth if he will return and repent, and leave a blessing behind him; even a meat offering and a drink offering unto the LORD your God?

Joel 2:13-14

But woe unto you, Pharisees! for ye tithe mint and rue and all manner of herbs, and pass over judgment and the love of God: these ought ye to have done, and not to leave the other undone.

Luke 11:42

As it is written, He that had gathered much had nothing over; and he that had gathered little had no lack.

II Corinthians 8:15

He that is faithful in that which is least is faithful also in much: and he that is unjust in the least is unjust also in much.

If therefore ye have not been faithful in the unrighteous mammon, who will commit to your trust the true riches?

Luke 16:10-11

Bring forth therefore fruits meet for repentance:

And think not to say within yourselves, We have Abraham to our father: for I say unto you, that God is able of these stones to raise up children unto Abraham.

Matthew 3:8-9

Doth he thank that servant because he did the things that were commanded him? I trow not.

So likewise ye, when ye shall have done all those things which are commanded you, say, We are unprofitable servants: we have done that which was our duty to do.

Luke 17:9-10

And as soon as the commandment came abroad, the children of Israel brought in abundance the firstfruits of corn, wine, and oil, and honey, and of all the increase of the field; and the tithe of all things brought they in abundantly.

II Chronicles 31:5

Hoping In Christ...

How To Commit Your Life To Christ

That if thou shalt confess with thy mouth the Lord Jesus, and shalt believe in thine heart that God hath raise him from the dead, thou shalt be saved.

For with the heart man believeth unto righteousness; and with the mouth confession is made unto salvation.

For the scripture saith, Whosoever believeth on him shall not be ashamed.

For there is no difference between the Jew and the Greek: for the same Lord over all is rich unto all that call upon him.

For whosoever shall call upon the name of the Lord shall be saved.

Romans 10:9-13

Trust in the LORD, and do good; so shalt thou dwell in the land, and verily thou shalt be fed.

Delight thyself also in the LORD; and he shall give thee the desires of thine heart.

Commit thy way unto the LORD; trust also in him; and he shall bring it to pass.

And he shall bring forth thy righteousness as the light, and thy judgment as the noonday.

Rest in the LORD, and wait patiently for him: fret not thyself because of him who prospereth in his way, because of the man who bringeth wicked devices to pass.

Psalm 37:3-7

Seek ye the LORD while he may be found, call ye upon him while he is near:

Let the wicked forsake his way, and the unrighteous man his thoughts: and let him return unto the LORD, and he will have mercy upon him; and to our God, for he will abundantly pardon.

Isaiah 55:6-7

Behold, I stand at the door, and knock: if any man hear my voice, and open the door, I will come in to him, and will sup with him, and he with him.

Revelation 3:20

All that the Father giveth me shall come to me; and him that cometh to me I will in no wise cast out.

And this is the will of him that sent me, the very one which seeth the Son, and believeth on him, may have everlasting life: and I will raise him up at the last day.

No man can come to me, except the Father which hath sent me draw him: and I will raise him up at the last day.

It is written in the prophets, And they shall be all taught of God. Every man therefore that hath heard, and hath learned of the Father, cometh unto me.

Not that any man hath seen the Father, save he which is of God, he hath seen the Father.

Verily, verily, I say unto you, He that believeth on me hath everlasing life.

John 6:37, 40, 44-47

But without faith it is impossible to please him; for he that cometh to God must believe that he is, and that he is a rewarder of them that diligently seek him.

Hebrews 11:6

A new heart also will I give you, and a new spirit will I put within you: and I will take away the stony heart out of your flesh, and I will give you an heart of flesh.

And I will put my spirit within you, and cause you to walk in my statutes, and ye shall keep my judgments, and do them.

Ezekiel 36:26-27

The Lord is not slack concerning his promise, as some men count slackness; but is longsuffering to us-ward, not willing that any should perish, but that all should come to repentance.

But grow in grace, and in the knowledge of our Lord and Saviour Jesus Christ. To him be glory both now and for ever. Amen.

II Peter 3:9, 18

Draw nigh to God, and he will draw nigh to you. Cleanse your hands, ye sinners; and purify your hearts, ye double-minded.

James 4:8

•

But now being made free from sin, and become servants to God, ye have your fruit unto holiness, and the end everlasting life.

For the wages of sin is death; but the gift of God is eternal life through Jesus Christ our Lord.

Romans 6:22-23

HAVE mercy upon me, O God, according to thy lovingkindness: according unto the multitude of thy tender mercies blot out my transgressions.

Wash me thoroughly from mine iniquity, and cleanse me from my sin.

For I acknowledge my transgressions: and my sin is ever before me.

Create in me a clean heart, O God; and renew a right spirit within me.

Cast me not away from thy presence; and take not thy holy spirit from me.

Restore unto me the joy of thy salvation; and uphold me with thy free spirit.

Psalm 51:1-3, 10-12

For the which cause I also suffer these things: nevertheless I am not ashamed: for I know whom I have believed, and am persuaded that he is able to keep that which I have committed unto him against that day.

II Timothy 1:12

Whosoever therefore shall confess me before men, him will I confess also before my Father which is in heaven.

And he that taketh not his cross, and followeth after me is not worthy of me.

He that findeth his life shall lose it: and he that loseth his life for my sake shall find it.

He that receiveth you receiveth me, and he that receiveth me receiveth him that sent me.

He that receiveth a prophet in the name of a prophet shall receive a prophet's reward; and he that receiveth a righteous man in the name of a righteous man shall receive a righteous man's reward.

And whosoever shall give to drink unto one of these little ones a cup of cold water only in the name of a disciple, verily I say unto you, he shall in no wise lose his reward.

Matthew 10:32, 38-42

Go to now, ye that say, Today or tomorrow we will go into such a city, and continue there a year, and buy and sell, and get gain:

Whereas ye know not what shall be on the morrow. For what is your life? It is even a vapour, that appeareth for a little time, and then vanisheth away.

For that ye ought to say, If the Lord will, we shall live, and do this, or that.

James 4:13-15

I tell you, Nay: but, except ye repent, ye shall all likewise perish.

Luke 13:3

The LORD is nigh unto all them that call upon him, to all that call upon him in truth.

He will fulfil the desire of them that fear him: he also will hear their cry, and will save them.

The LORD preserveth all them that love him: but all the wicked will he destroy.

My mouth shall speak the praise of the LORD: and let all flesh bless his holy name for ever and ever.

Psalm 145:18-21

How To Draw Nigh To God

Draw nigh to God, and he will draw nigh to you. Cleanse your hands, ye sinners; and purify your hearts, ye double-minded.

Be afflicted, and mourn, and weep: let your laughter be turned to mourning, and your joy to heaviness.

Humble yourselves in the sight of the Lord, and he shall lift you up.

James 4:8-10

I love them that love me; and those that seek me early shall find me.

Proverbs 8:17

And I say unto you, Ask, and it shall be given you; seek, and ye shall find; knock, and it shall be opened unto you.

For every one that asketh receiveth; and he that seeketh findeth; and to him that knocketh it shall be opened.

If a son shall ask bread of any of you that is a father, will he give him a stone? or if he ask a fish, will he for a fish give him a serpent?

Or if he shall ask an egg, will he offer him a scorpion?

If ye then, being evil, know how to give good gifts unto your children: how much more shall your heavenly Father give the Holy Spirit to them that ask him?

Luke 11:9-13

Seek the LORD and his strength, seek his face continually.

Remember his marvellous works that he hath done, his wonders, and the judgments of his mouth;

I Chronicles 16:11-12

Then shall ye call upon me, and ye shall go and pray unto me, and I will hearken unto you.

And ye shall seek me, and find me, when ye shall search for me with all your heart.

Jeremiah 29:12-13

As the hart panteth after the water brooks, so panteth my soul after thee, O God.

My soul thirsteth for God, for the living God: when shall I come and appear before God?

Deep calleth unto deep at the noise of thy waterspouts: all thy waves and thy billows are gone over me.

Yet the LORD will command his lovingkindness in the daytime, and in the night his song shall be with me, and my prayer unto the God of my life.

Psalm 42:1-2, 7-8

BLESSED are they that keep his testimonies, and that seek him with the whole heart.

With my whole heart have I sought thee: O let me not wander from thy commandments.

Psalm 119:2, 10

I wait for the LORD, my soul doth wait, and in his word do I hope.

My soul waiteth for the Lord more than they that watch for the morning: I say, more than they that watch for the morning.

Psalm 130:5-6

The LORD is nigh unto all them that call upon him, to all that call upon him in truth.

Psalm 145:18

In my distress I called upon the LORD, and cried unto my God: he heard my voice out of his temple, and my cry came before him, even into his ears.

Psalm 18:6

In the day when I cried thou answeredst me, and strengthenedst me with strength in my soul.

Psalm 138:3

Thus will I bless thee while I live: I will lift up my hands in thy name.

My soul shall be satisfied as with marrow and fatness; and my mouth shall praise thee with joyful lips:

Psalm 63:4-5

My soul, wait thou only upon God; for my expectation is from him.

Psalm 62:5

HEAR my cry, O God; attend unto my prayer.

From the end of the earth will I cry unto thee, when my heart is overwhelmed: lead me to the rock that is higher than I.

Psalm 61:1-2

All that the Father giveth me shall come to me; and him that cometh to me I will in no wise cast out.

John 6:37

And the Spirit and the bride say, Come. And let him that heareth say, Come. And let him that is athirst come. And whosoever will, let him take the water of life freely.

Revelation 22:17

How To Recover Spiritually

Hast thou not known? hast thou not heard, that the everlasting God, the LORD, the Creator of the ends of the earth, fainteth not, neither is weary? there is no searching of his understanding.

He giveth power to the faint; and to them that have no might he increaseth strength.

But they that wait upon the LORD shall renew their strength; they shall mount up with wings as eagles; they shall run, and not be weary; and they shall walk, and not faint.

Isaiah 40:28-29, 31

For thou, Lord, art good, and ready to forgive; and plenteous in mercy unto all them that call upon thee.

Give ear, O LORD, unto my prayer; and attend to the voice of my supplications.

In the day of my trouble I will call upon thee: for thou wilt answer me.

Psalm 86:5-7

Brethren, I count not myself to have apprehended: but this one thing I do, forgetting those things which are behind, and reaching forth unto those things which are before,

I press toward the mark for the prize of the high calling of God in Christ Jesus.

Philippians 3:13-14

I will seek that which was lost, and bring again that which was driven away, and will bind up that which was broken, and will strengthen that which was sick: but I will destroy the fat and the strong; I will feed them with judgment.

Thus shall they know that I the LORD their God am with them, and that they, even the house of Israel, are my people, saith the Lord GOD.

And ye my flock, the flock of my pasture, are men, and I am your God, saith the Lord GOD.

Ezekiel 34:16, 30-31

He that covereth his sins shall not prosper: but whoso confesseth and forsaketh them shall have mercy.

Proverbs 28:13

Before I was afflicted I went astray: but now have I kept thy word.

Thou art good, and doest good; teach me thy statutes.

Psalm 119:67-68

Now no chastening for the present seemeth to be joyous, but grievous: nevertheless afterward it yieldeth the peaceable fruit of righteousness unto them which are exercised thereby.

Wherefore lift up the hands which hang down, and the feeble knees;

And make straight paths for your feet, lest that which is lame be turned out of the way; but let it rather be healed.

Follow peace with all men, and holiness, without which no man shall see the Lord:

Hebrews 12:11-14

Take away the dross from the silver, and there shall come forth a vessel for the finer.

Proverbs 25:4

The righteous shall flourish like the palm tree: he shall grow like a cedar in Lebanon.

Those that be planted in the house of the LORD shall flourish in the courts of our God.

They shall still bring forth fruit in old age; they shall be fat and flourising;

To shew that the LORD is upright: he is my rock, and there is no unrighteousness in him.

Psalm 92:12-15

Blessed is the man whom thou chastenest, O LORD and teachest him out of thy law;

That thou mayest give him rest from the days of adversity, until the pit be digged for the wicked.

For the LORD will not cast off his people, neither will he forsake his inheritance.

Psalm 94:12-14

I will heal their backsliding, I will love them freely: for mine anger is turned away from him.

Hosea 14:4

Poverty and shame shall be to him that refuseth instruction: but he that regardeth reproof shall be honoured.

Proverbs 13:18

But speaking the truth in love, may grow up into him in all things, which is the head, even Christ:

From whom the whole body fitly joined together and compacted by that which every joint supplieth, according to the effectual working in the measure of every part, maketh increase of the body unto the edifying of itself in love.

Ephesians 4:15-16

When my soul fainted within me I remembered the LORD: and my prayer came in unto thee, into thine holy temple.

They that observe lying vanities forsake their own mercy.

But I will sacrifice unto thee with the voice of thanksgiving; I will pay that that I have vowed. Salvation is of the LORD.

Jonah 2:7-9

I cried unto thee, O LORD: I said, Thou art my refuge and my portion in the land of the living.

Attend unto my cry; for I am brought very low: deliver me from my persecutors; for they are stronger than I.

Bring my soul out of prison, that I may praise thy name: the righteous shall compass me about; for thou shalt deal bountifully with me.

Psalm 142:5-7

How To Obtain The Promises

Whereby are given unto us exceeding great and precious promises: that by these ye might be partakers of the divine nature, having escaped the corruption that is in the world through lust.

And beside this, giving all diligence, add to your faith virtue; and to virtue knowledge;

And to knowledge temperance; and to temperance patience; and to patience godliness;

And to godliness brotherly kindness; and to brotherly kindness charity.

For if these things be in you, and abound, they make you that ye shall neither be barren nor unfruitful in the knowledge of our Lord Jesus Christ.

II Peter 1:4-8

Let us hold fast the profession of our faith without wavering; (for he is faithful that promised;)

Cast not away therefore your confidence, which hath great recompence of reward.

For ye have need of patience, that, after ye have done the will of God, ye might receive the promise.

For yet a little while, and he that shall come will come, and will not tarry.

Hebrew 10:23, 35-37

For if ye shall diligently keep all these commandments which I command you, to do them, to love the LORD your God, to walk in all his ways, and to cleave unto him;

Then will the LORD drive out all these nations from before you, and ye shall possess greater nations and mightier than yourselves.

Deuteronomy 11:22-23

Only be thou strong and very courageous, that thou mayest observe to do according to all the law, which Moses my servant commanded thee: turn not from it to the right hand or to the left, that thou mayest prosper whithersoever thou goest.

Joshua 1:7

For verily I say unto you, That whosoever shall say unto this mountain, Be thou removed, and be thou cast into the sea; and shall not doubt in his heart, but shall believe that those things which he saith shall come to pass; he shall have whatsoever he saith.

Mark 11:23

Now faith is the substance of things hoped for, the evidence of things not seen.

But without faith it is impossible to please him: for he that cometh to God must believe that he is, and that he is a rewarder of them that diligently seek him.

Through faith also Sarah herself received strength to conceive seed, and was delivered of a child when she was past age, because she judged him faithful who had promised.

Hebrews 11:1, 6, 11

That ye be not slothful, but followers of them who through faith and patience inherit the promises.

Hebrews 6:12

For ye are all the children of God by faith in Christ Jesus.

For as many of you as have been baptized into Christ have put on Christ.

There is neither Jew nor Greek, there is neither bond nor free, there is neither male nor female: for ye are all one in Christ Jesus.

And if ye be Christ's, then are ye Abraham's seed, and heirs according to the promise.

Galatians 3:26-29

If ye be willing and obedient, ye shall eat the good of the land:

But if ye refuse and rebel, ye shall be devoured with the sword: for the mouth of the LORD hath spoken it.

Isaiah 1:19-20

Therefore it is of faith, that it might be by grace; to the end the promise might be sure to all the seed; not to that only which is of the law, but to that also which is of the faith of Abraham; who is the father of us all,

Romans 4:16

And this is the confidence that we have in him, that, if we ask any thing according to his will, he heareth us:

And if we know that he hear us, whatsoever we ask, we know that we have the petitions that we desired of him.

I John 5:14-15

And said, If thou wilt diligently hearken to the voice of the LORD thy God, and wilt do that which is right in his sight, and wilt give ear to his commandments, and keep all his statutes, I will put none of these diseases upon thee, which I have brought upon the Egyptians: for I am the LORD that healeth thee.

Exodus 15:26

If any of you lack wisdom, let him ask of God, that giveth to all men liberally, and upbraideth not; and it shall be given him.

But let him ask in faith, nothing wavering. For he that wavereth is like a wave of the sea driven with the wind and tossed.

For let not that man think that he shall receive any thing of the Lord.

A double-minded man is unstable in all his ways.

James 1:5-8

For with God nothing shall be impossible.

Luke 1:37

BEHOLD, the LORD'S hand is not shortened, that it cannot save; neither his ear heavy, that it cannot hear:

But your iniquities have separated between you and your God, and your sins have hid his face from you, that he will not hear.

Isaiah 59:1-2

But seek ye first the kingdom of God, and his righteousness; and all these things shall be added unto you.

Matthew 6:33

Understanding In Christ . . .

How To Understand The Personality of God

As for God, his way is perfect: the word of the Lord is tried: he is a buckler to all those that trust in him.

For who is God save the LORD? Or who is a rock save our God?

It is God that girdeth me with strength, and maketh my way perfect.

Psalm 18:30-32

For my thoughts are not your thoughts, neither are your ways my ways, saith the LORD.

For as the heavens are higher than the earth, so are my ways higher than your ways, and my thoughts than your thoughts.

Isaiah 55:8-9

Though the LORD be high, yet hath he respect unto the lowly: but the proud he knoweth afar off.

Though I walk in the midst of trouble, thou wilt revive me: thou shalt stretch forth thine hand against the wrath of mine enemies, and thy right hand shall save me.

Psalm 138:6-7

Every good gift and every perfect gift is from above, and cometh down from the Father of lights, with whom is no variableness, neither shadow of turning.

James 1:17

I the LORD search the heart, I try the reins, even to give every man according to his ways, and according to the fruit of his doings.

Jeremiah 17:10

He hath made the earth by his power, he hath established the world by his wisdom, and hath stretched out the heavens by his discretion.

Jeremiah 10:12

The LORD is in his holy temple, the LORD'S throne is in heaven: his eyes behold, his eyelids try, the children of men.

The LORD trieth the righteous: but the wicked and him that loveth violence his soul hateth.

For the righteous LORD loveth righteousness: his countenance doth behold the upright.

Psalm 11:4-5, 7

Wherefore now let the fear of the LORD be upon you; take heed and do it: for there is no iniquity with the LORD our God, nor respect of persons, nor taking of gifts.

II Chronicles 19:7

I know that thou canst do every thing, and that no thought can be withholden from thee.

Job 42:2

And all the trees of the field shall know that I the LORD have brought down the high tree, have exalted the low tree, have dried up the green tree, and have made the dry tree to flourish: I the LORD have spoken and have done it.

Ezekiel 17:24

Jesus saith unto them, Did ye never read in the scriptures, The stone which the builders rejected, the same is become the head of the corner: this is the Lord's doing, and it is marvellous in our eyes?

Matthew 21:42

Like as a father pitieth his children, so the LORD pitieth them that fear him.

For he knoweth our frame; he remembereth that we are dust.

Psalm 103:13-14

If ye then, being evil, know how to give good gifts unto your children, how much more shall your Father which is in heaven give good things to them that ask him?

Matthew 7:11

But glory, honour, and peace, to every man that worketh good, to the Jew first, and also to the Gentile:

For there is no respect of persons with God.

Romans 2:10-11

Because the foolishness of God is wiser than men; and the weakness of God is stronger than men.

I Corinthians 1:25

Great is our Lord, and of great power: his understanding is infinite.

Psalm 147:5

Great is the LORD, and greatly to be praised; and his greatness is unsearchable.

The LORD is gracious, and full of compassion; slow to anger, and of great mercy.

The LORD is good to all: and his tender mercies are over all his works.

Psalm 145:3, 8-9

Wherefore we receiving a kingdom which cannot be moved, let us have grace, whereby we may serve God acceptably with reverence and godly fear:

For our God is a consuming fire.

Hebrews 12:28-29

If we confess our sins, he is faithful and just to forgive us our sins, and to cleanse us from all unrighteousness.

I John 1:9

For his anger endureth but a moment; in his favour is life: weeping may endure for a night, but joy cometh in the morning.

Psalm 30:5

So he fed them according to the integrity of his heart; and guided them by the skilfulness of his hands.

Psalm 78:72

After that he poureth water into a basin, and began to wash the disciples' feet, and to wipe them with the towel wherewith he was girded.

If I then, your, Lord and Master, have washed your feet; ye also ought to wash one another's feet.

John 13:5, 14

How To Receive Understanding

The fear of the LORD is the beginning of wisdom: a good understanding have all they that do his commandments: his praise endureth for ever.

Psalm 111:10

Counsel is mine, and sound wisdom: I am understanding; I have strength.

Proverbs 8:14

Understanding is a wellspring of life unto him that hath it: but the instruction of fools is folly.

Proverbs 16:22

Forsake the foolish, and live; and go in the way of understanding.

The fear of the LORD is the beginning of wisdom: and the knowledge of the holy is understanding.

Proverbs 9:6, 10

How much better is it to get wisdom than gold! and to get understanding rather to be chosen than silver!

The highway of the upright is to depart from evil: he that keepeth his way preserveth his soul.

Proverbs 16:16-17

Surely the Lord GOD will do nothing, but he revealeth his secret unto his servants the prophets.

The lion hath roared, who will not fear? the Lord GOD hath spoken, who can but prophesy?

Amos 3:7-8

If any of you lack wisdom, let him ask of God, that giveth to all men liberally, and upbraideth not; and it shall be given him.

James 1:5

Make me to understand the way of thy precepts: so shall I talk of thy wondrous works.

Give me understanding, and I shall keep thy law; yea, I shall observe it with my whole heart.

Thy hands have made me and fashioned me: give me understanding, that I may learn thy commandments.

Thou through thy commandments hast made me wiser than mine enemies: for they are ever with me.

Through thy precepts I get understanding: therefore I hate every false way.

Thy word is a lamp unto my feet, and a light unto my path.

I am thy servant; give me understanding, that I may know thy testimonies.

Psalm 119: 27, 34, 73, 98, 104, 105, 125

Yea, if thou criest after knowledge, and liftest up thy voice for understanding;

If thou seekest her as silver, and searchest for her as for hid treasures;

Then shalt thou understand the fear of the LORD, and find the knowledge of God.

For the LORD giveth wisdom: out of his mouth cometh knowledge and understanding.

He layeth up sound wisdom for the righteous: he is a buckler to them that walk uprightly.

He keepeth the paths of judgment, and preserveth the way of his saints.

Then shalt thou understand righteousness, and judgment, and equity; yea, every good path.

When wisdom entereth into thine heart, and knowledge is pleasant unto thy soul;

Discretion shall preserve thee, understanding shall keep thee:

Proverbs 2:3-11

Get wisdom, get understanding: forget it not; neither decline from the words of my mouth.

For sake her not, and she shall preserve thee: love her, and she shall keep thee.

Wisdom is the principal thing; therefore get wisdom: and with all thy getting get understanding.

Proverbs 4:5-7

The heart of him that hath understanding seeketh knowledge: but the mouth of fools feedeth on foolishness.

Folly is joy to him that is destitute of wisdom: but a man of understanding walketh uprightly.

He that refuseth instruction despiseth his own soul: but he that heareth reproof getteth understanding.

The fear of the LORD is the instruction of wisdom; and before honour is humility.

Proverbs 15:14, 21, 32-33

For what man knoweth the things of a man, save the spirit of man which is in him? even so the things of God knoweth no man, but the Spirit of God.

Now we have received, not the spirit of the world, but the spirit which is of God; that we might know the things that are freely given to us of God.

Which things also we speak, not in the words which man's wisdom teacheth, but which the Holy Ghost teacheth; comparing spiritual things with spiritual.

I Corinthians 2:11-13

Incline your ear, and come unto me: hear, and your soul shall live; and I will make an everlasting covenant with you, even the sure mercies of David.

Seek ye the LORD while he may be found, call ye upon him while he is near:

For my thoughts are not your thoughts, neither are your ways my ways, saith the LORD.

For as the heavens are higher than the earth, so are my ways higher than your ways, and my thoughts than your thoughts.

Isaiah 55:3, 6, 8-9

But there is a spirit in man: and the inspiration of the Almighty giveth them understanding.

Job 32:8

What Is The Fear Of The Lord?

The LORD is righteous in all his ways, and holy in all his works.

The LORD is nigh unto all them that call upon him, to all that call upon him in truth.

He will fulfil the desire of them that fear him: he also will hear their cry, and will save them.

Psalm 145:17-19

He delighteth not in the strength of the horse: he taketh not pleasure in the legs of a man.

The LORD taketh pleasure in them that fear him, in those that hope in his mercy.

Psalm 147:10-11

If thou seekest her as silver, and searchest for her as for hid treasures;

Then shalt thou understand the fear of the LORD, and find the knowledge of God.

Proverbs 2:4-5

The fear of the LORD is the beginning of wisdom: and the knowledge of the holy is understanding.

Proverbs 9:10

All the days of the afflicted are evil: but he that is of a merry heart hath a continual feast.

The fear of the LORD is the instruction of wisdom; and before honour is humility.

Proverbs 15:15, 33

The fear of the LORD is the beginning of knowledge: but fools despise wisdom and instruction.

Proverbs 1:7

The fear of the LORD tendeth to life: and he that hath it shall abide satisfied; he shall not be visited with evil.

Proverbs 19:23

Then they that feared the LORD spake often one to another: and the LORD hearkened, and heard it, and a book of remembrance was written before him for them that feared the LORD, and that thought upon his name.

And they shall be mine, saith the LORD of hosts, in that day when I make up my jewels; and I will spare them, as a man spareth his own son that serveth him.

Malachi 3:16-17

In the fear of the LORD is strong confidence: and his children shall have a place of refuge.

The fear of the LORD is a fountain of life, to depart from the snares of death.

Proverbs 14:26-27

The fear of the LORD prolongeth days: but the years of the wicked shall be shortened.

Proverbs 10:27

And unto man he said, Behold, the fear of the Lord, that is wisdom; and to depart from evil is understanding.

Job 28:28

What man is he that feareth the LORD? him shall he teach in the way that he shall choose.

His soul shall dwell at ease; and his seed shall inherit the earth.

The secret of the LORD is with them that fear him; and he will shew them his covenant.

Psalm 25:12-14

For great is the LORD, and greatly to be praised: he also is to be feared above all gods.

I Chronicles 16:25

By mercy and truth iniquity is purged: and by the fear of the LORD men depart from evil.

Proverbs 16:6

The fear of the LORD is clean, enduring for ever: the judgments of the LORD are true and righteous altogether.

Psalm 19:9

O fear the LORD, ye his saints: for there is no want to them that fear him.

Psalm 34:9

PRAISE ye the LORD. Blessed is the man that feareth the LORD, that delighteth greatly in his commandments.

Psalm 112:1

Let us hear the conclusion of the whole matter: Fear God, and keep his commandments: for this is the whole duty of man.

For God shall bring every work into judgment, with every secret thing, whether it be good, or whether it be evil.

Ecclesiastes 12:13-14

What Is The Sovereignty Of God?

Great is the LORD, and greatly to be praised; and his greatness is unsearchable.

One generation shall praise thy works to another, and shall declare thy mighty acts.

Thy kingdom is an everlasting kingdom, and thy dominion endureth throughout all generations.

Psalms 145:3-4, 13

All nations before him are as nothing; and they are counted to him less than nothing, and vanity.

To whom then will ye liken God? or what likeness will ye compare unto him?

To whom then will ye liken me, or shall I be equal? saith the Holy One.

Lift up your eyes on high, and behold who hath created these things, that bringeth out their host by number: he calleth them all by names by the greatness of his might, for that he is strong in power; not one faileth.

Hast thou not known? hast thou not heard, that the everlasting God, the LORD, the Creator of the ends of the earth, fainteth not, neither is weary? there is no searching of his understanding.

Isaiah 40:17, 18, 25, 26, 28

THUS saith the LORD, The heaven is my throne, and the earth is my footstool: where is the house that ye build unto me? and where is the place of my rest?

For all those things hath mine hand made, and all those things have been, saith the LORD: but to this man will I look, even to him that is poor and of a contrite spirit, and trembleth at my word.

Isaiah 66:1-2

For the LORD is our judge, the LORD is our lawgiver, the LORD is our king; he will save us.

Isaiah 33:22

And Moses said unto God, Behold, when I come unto the children of Israel, and shall say unto them, The God of your fathers hath sent me unto you; and they shall say to me, What is his name? what shall I say unto them?

And God said unto Moses, I AM THAT I AM: and he said, Thus shalt thou say unto the children of Israel, I AM hath sent me unto you.

Exodus 3:13-14

For with God nothing shall be impossible.

Luke 1:37

LORD, thou hast been our dwelling place in all generations.

Before the mountains were brought forth, or ever thou hadst formed the earth and the world, even from everlasting to everlasting, thou art God.

Thou turnest man to destruction; and sayest, Return, ye children of men.

For a thousand years in thy sight are but as yesterday when it is past, and as a watch in the night.

Psalm 90:1-4

See now that I, even I, am he, and there is no god with me: I kill, and I make alive; I wound, and I heal: neither is there any that can deliver out of my hand.

For I lift up my hand to heaven, and say, I live for ever.

Deuteronomy 32:39-40

Where wast thou when I laid the foundations of the earth? declare, if thou hast understanding.

Who hath laid the measures thereof, if thou knowest? Or who hath stretched the line upon it?

Whereupon are the foundations thereof fastened? Or who laid the corner stone thereof;

When the morning stars sang together, and all the sons of God shouted for joy?

Job 38:4-7

Whom have I in heaven but thee? and there is none upon earth that I desire beside thee.

Psalm 73:25

This is the purpose that is purposed upon the whole earth: and this is the hand that is stretched out upon all the nations.

For the LORD of hosts hath purposed, and who shall disannul it? and his hand is stretched out, and who shall turn it back?

Isaiah 14:26-27

For thus saith the high and lofty One that inhabiteth eternity, whose name is Holy; I dwell in the high and holy place, with him also that is of a contrite and humble spirit, to revive the spirit of the humble, and to revive the heart of the contrite ones.

Isaiah 57:15

Am I a God at hand, saith the LORD, and not a God afar off?

Can any hide himself in secret places that I shall not see him? saith the LORD. Do not I fill heaven and earth? saith the LORD.

Jeremiah 23:23-24

And when I saw him, I fell at his feet as dead. And he laid his right hand upon me, saying unto me, Fear not; I am the first and the last:

I am he that liveth, and was dead; and, behold, I am alive for evermore, Amen; and have the keys of hell and of death.

Revelation 1:17-18

The heavens declare the glory of God; and the firmament sheweth his handiwork.

Psalm 19:1

Behold, I am the LORD, the God of all flesh: is there any thing too hard for me?

Jeremiah 32:27

IN the beginning God created the heaven and the earth.

And the earth was without form, and void; and darkness was upon the face of the deep. And the spirit of God moved upon the face of the waters.

And God said, Let there be light: and there was light.

Genesis 1:1-3

UNDERSTANDING IN CHRIST

How To Grasp Eternity

And I heard a great voice out of heaven saying, Behold, the tabernacle of God is with men, and he will dwell with them, and they shall be his people, and God himself shall be with them, and be their God.

And God shall wipe away all tears from their eyes; and there shall be no more death, neither sorrow, nor crying, neither shall there be any more pain: for the former things are passed away.

And he that sat upon the throne said, Behold, I make all things new. And he said unto me, Write: for these words are true and faithful.

And he said unto me, It is done. I am Alpha and Omega, the beginning and the end. I will give unto him that is athirst of the fountain of the water of life freely.

Revelation 21:3-6

But as it is written, Eye hath not seen, nor ear heard, neither have entered into the heart of man, the things which God hath prepared for them that love him.

But God hath revealed them unto us by his Spirit: for the spirit searcheth all things, yea, the deep things of God.

For what man knoweth the things of a man, save the spirit of man which is in him? even so the things of God knoweth no man, but the Spirit of God.

I Corinthians 2:9-11

Violence shall no more be heard in thy land, wasting nor destruction within thy borders; but thou shalt call thy walls Salvation, and thy gates Praise.

The sun shall be no more thy light by day; neither for brightness shall the moon give light unto thee: but the LORD shall be unto thee an everlasting light, and thy God thy glory.

Thy sun shall no more go down; neither shall thy moon withdraw itself: for the LORD shall be thine everlasting light, and the days of thy mourning shall be ended.

Isaiah 60:18-20

And the city had no need of the sun, neither of the moon, to shine in it: for the glory of God did lighten it, and the Lamb is the light thereof.

And the nations of them which are saved shall walk in the light of it: and the kings of the earth do bring their glory and honour into it.

And the gates of it shall not be shut at all by day: for there shall be no night there.

And they shall bring the glory and honour of the nations into it.

And there shall in no wise enter into it any thing that defileth, neither whatsoever worketh abomination, or maketh a lie: but they which are written in the Lamb's book of life.

Revelation 21:23-27

So when this corruptible shall have put on incorruption, and this mortal shall have put on immortality, then shall be brought to pass the saying that is written, Death is swallowed up in victory.

O death, where is thy sting? O Grave, where is thy victory?

But thanks be to God, which giveth us the victory through our Lord Jesus Christ.

I Corinthians 15:54, 55, 57

I saw in the night visions, and, behold, one like the Son of man came with the clouds of heaven, and came to the Ancient of days, and they brought him near before him.

And there was given him dominion, and glory, and a kingdom, that all people, nations, and languages, should serve him: his dominion is an everlasting dominion, which shall not pass away, and his kingdom that which shall not be destroyed.

Daniel 7:13-14

There are also celestial bodies, and bodies terrestrial: but the glory of the celestial is one, and the glory of the terrestrial is another.

So also is the resurrection of the dead. It is sown in corruption; it is raised in incorruption:

It is sown in dishonour; it is raised in glory: it is sown in weakness; it is raised in power:

It is sown a natural body; it is raised a spiritual body. There is a natural body, and there is a spiritual body.

I Corinthians 15:40, 42-44

And they that be wise shall shine as the brightness of the firmament; and they that turn many to righteousness as the stars for ever and ever.

Daniel 12:3

For now we see through a glass, darkly; but then face to face: now I know in part; but then shall I know even as also I am known.

I Corinthians 13:12

Verily I say unto you, I will drink no more of the fruit of the vine, until that day that I drink it new in the kingdom of God.

Mark 14:25

He will swallow up death in victory; and the Lord GOD will wipe away tears from off all faces; and the rebuke of his people shall he take away from off all the earth: for the LORD hath spoken it.

Isaiah 25:8

Surely goodness and mercy shall follow me all the days of my life; and I will dwell in the house of the LORD for ever.

Psalm 23:6

And when I saw him, I fell at his feet as dead. And he laid his right hand upon me, saying unto me, Fear not; I am the first and the last:

I am he that liveth, and was dead; and, behold, I am alive for evermore, Amen; and have the keys of hell and of death.

Revelation 1:17-18

For since the beginning of the world men have not heard, nor perceived by the ear, neither hath the eye seen, O God, beside thee, what he hath prepared for him that waiteth for him.

Isaiah 64:4

Uniting In Christ...

What Is The Fellowship Of All Believers?

But now hath God set the members every one of them in the body, as it hath pleased him.

And if they were all one member, where were the body?

But now are they many members, yet but one body.

And the eye cannot say unto the hand, I have no need of thee: nor again the head to the feet, I have no need of you.

Nay, much more those members of the body, which seem to be more feeble, are necessary:

And those members of the body, which we think to be less honourable, upon these we bestow more abundant honour; and our uncomely parts have more abundant comeliness.

For our comely parts have no need: but God hath tempered the body together, having given more abundant honour to that part which lacked:

That there should be no schism in the body; but that the members should have the same care one for another.

And whether one member suffer, all the members suffer with it; or one member be honoured, all the members rejoice with it.

Now ye are the body of Christ, and members in particular.

I Corinthians 12:18-27

Now therefore ye are no more strangers and foreigners, but fellow citizens with the saints, and of the household of God;

And are built upon the foundation of the apostles and prophets, Jesus Christ himself being the chief corner stone;

In whom all the building fitly framed together groweth unto a holy temple in the Lord:

In whom ye also are builded together for an habitation of God through the Spirit.

Ephesians 2:19-22

Finally, be ye all of one mind, having compassion one of another, love as brethren, be pitiful, be courteous:

Not rendering evil for evil, or railing for railing: but contrariwise blessing; knowing that ye are thereunto called, that ye should inherit a blessing.

I Peter 3:8-9

For where two or three are gathered together in my name, there am I in the midst of them.

Then came Peter to him, and said, Lord, how oft shall my brother sin against me, and I forgive him? till seven times?

Jesus saith unto him, I say not unto thee, Until seven times: but, Until seventy times seven.

Matthew 18:20-22

He that saith he is in the light, and hateth his brother, is in darkness even until now.

He that loveth his brother abideth in the light, and there is none occasion of stumbling in him.

But he that hateth his brother is in darkness, and walketh in darkness, and knoweth not whither he goeth, because that darkness hath blinded his eyes.

I John 2:9-11

God is faithful, by whom ye were called unto the fellowship of his Son Jesus Christ our Lord.

Now I beseech you, brethren, by the name of our Lord Jesus Christ, that ye all speak the same thing, and that there be no divisions among you; but that ye be perfectly joined together in the same mind and in the same judgment.

I Corinthians 1:9-10

For ye are yet carnal: for whereas there is among you envying, and strife, and divisions, are ye not carnal, and walk as men?

For while one saith, I am of Paul; and another, I am of Apollos; are ye not carnal?

Who then is Paul, and who is Apollos, but ministers by whom ye believed, even as the Lord gave to every man?

I have planted, Apollos watered; but God gave the increase.

So then neither is he that planteth any thing, neither he that watereth; but God that giveth the increase.

Now he that planteth and he that watereth are one: and every man shall receive his own reward according to his own labour.

For we are labourers together with God: ye are God's husbandry, ye are God's building.

I Corinthians 3:3-9

Ye call me Master and Lord: and ye say well; for so I am.

If I then, your Lord and Master, have washed your feet; ye also ought to wash one another's feet.

For I have given you an example, that ye should do as I have done to you.

Verily, verily, I say unto you, The servant is not greater than his lord; neither he that is sent greater than he that sent him.

If ye know these things, happy are ye if ye do them.

John 13:13-17

Neither pray I for these alone, but for them also which shall believe on me through their word;

That they all may be one; as thou, Father, art in me, and I in thee, that they also may be one in us: that the world may believe that thou hast sent me.

And the glory which thou gavest me I have given them; that they may be one, even as we are one:

I in them, and thou in me, that they may be made perfect in one; and that the world may know that thou hast sent me, and hast loved them, as thou hast loved me.

John 17:20-23

And John answered him, saying, Master, we saw one casting out devils in thy name, and he followeth not us: and we forbade him, because he followeth not us.

But Jesus said, Forbid him not: for there is no man which shall do a miracle in my name, that can lightly speak evil of me.

For he that is not against us is on our part.

For whosoever shall give you a cup of water to drink in my name, because ye belong to Christ, verily I say unto you, he shall not lose his reward.

And whosoever shall offend one of these little ones that believe in me, it is better for him that a millstone were hanged about his neck, and he were cast into the sea.

Mark 9:38-42

Ye also, as lively stones, are built up a spiritual house, an holy priesthood, to offer up spiritual sacrifices, acceptable to God by Jesus Christ.

But ye are a chosen generation, a royal priesthood, an holy nation, a peculiar people; that ye should shew forth the praises of him who hath called you out of darkness into his marvellous light:

I Peter 2:5, 9

But God, who is rich in mercy, for his great love wherewith he loved us,

Even when we were dead in sins hath quickened us together with Christ, (by grace ye are saved;)

And hath raised us up together, and made us sit together in heavenly places in Christ Jesus:

Ephesians 2:4-6

If we say that we have fellowship with him, and walk in darkness, we lie, and do not the truth:

But if we walk in the light, as he is in the light, we have fellowship one with another, and the blood of Jesus Christ his Son cleanseth us from all sin.

I John 1:6-7

BEHOLD, how good and how pleasant it is for brethren to dwell together in unity!

It is like the precious ointment upon the head, that ran down upon the beard, even Aaron's beard: that went down to the skirts of his garments;

As the dew of Hermon, and as the dew that descended upon the mountains of Zion: for there the LORD commanded the blessing, even life for evermore.

Psalm 133:1-3

He that is not with me is against me; and he that gathereth not with me scattereth abroad.

Matthew 12:30

And he stretched forth his hand toward his disciples, and said, Behold my mother and my brethren!

For whosoever shall do the will of my Father which is in heaven, the same is my brother, and sister, and mother.

Matthew 12:49-50

What? Know ye not that your body is the temple of the Holy Ghost which is in you, which ye have of God, and ye are not your own?

For ye are bought with a price: therefore glorify God in your body, and in your spirit, which are God's.

I Corinthians 6:19-20

There is neither Jew nor Greek, there is neither bond nor free, there is neither male nor female: for ye are all one in Christ Jesus.

And if ye be Christ's, then are ye Abraham's seed, and heirs according to the promise.

Galatians 3:28-29

But ye shall receive power, after that the Holy Ghost is come upon you: and ye shall be witnesses unto me both in Jerusalem, and in all Judaea, and in Samaria, and unto the uttermost part of the earth.

Acts 1:8

What Is The Hope For Revival?

The Lord is not slack concerning his promise, as some men count slackness; but is longsuffering to us-ward, not willing that any should perish, but that all should come to repentance.

II Peter 3:9

ARISE, shine; for thy light is come, and the glory of the LORD is risen upon thee.

For, behold, the darkness shall cover the earth, and gross darkness the people: but the LORD shall arise upon thee, and his glory shall be seen upon thee.

Isaiah 60:1-2

And they shall build the old wastes, they shall raise up the former desolations, and they shall repair the waste cities, the desolations of many generations.

For as the earth bringeth forth her bud, and as the garden causeth the things that are sown in it to spring forth; so the Lord GOD will cause righteousness and praise to spring forth before all the nations.

Isaiah 61:4,11

The voice of him that crieth in the wilderness, Prepare ye the way of the LORD, make straight in the desert a highway for our God.

Every valley shall be exalted, and every mountain and hill shall be made low: and the crooked shall be made straight, and the rough places plain:

And the glory of the LORD shall be revealed, and all flesh shall see it together for the mouth of the LORD hath spoken it.

Isaiah 40:3-5

All the ends of the world shall remember and turn unto the LORD: and all the kindreds of the nations shall worship before thee.

For the kingdom is the LORD'S: and he is the governor among the nations.

Psalm 22:27-28

Be patient therefore, brethren, unto the coming of the Lord. Behold, the husbandman waiteth for the precious fruit of the earth, and hath long patience for it, until he receive the early and latter rain.

James 5:7

And it shall come to pass afterward, that I will pour out my spirit upon all flesh; and your sons and your daughters shall prophesy, your old men shall dream dreams, your young men shall see visions:

And also upon the servants and upon the handmaids in those days will I pour out my spirit.

And I will shew wonders in the heavens and in the earth, blood, and fire, and pillars of smoke.

The sun shall be turned into darkness, and the moon into blood, before the great and the terrible day of the LORD come.

And it shall come to pass, that whosoever shall call on the name of the LORD shall be delivered: for in mount Zion and in Jerusalem shall be deliverance, as the LORD hath said, and in the remnant whom the LORD shall call.

Joel 2:28-32

And the Spirit and the bride say, Come. And let him that heareth say, Come. And let him that is athirst come. And whosoever will, let him take the water of life freely.

Revelation 22:17

For the earth shall be filled with the knowledge of the glory of the LORD, as the waters cover the sea.

Habakkuk 2:14

The LORD hath made bare his holy arm in the eyes of all the nations; and all the ends of the earth shall see the salvation of our God.

So shall he sprinkle many nations; the kings shall shut their mouths at him: for that which had not been told them shall they see; and that which they had not heard shall they consider.

Isaiah 52:10, 15

And this gospel of the kingdom shall be preached in all the world for a witness unto all nations; and then shall the end come.

Matthew 24:14

For the vision is yet for an appointed time, but at the end it shall speak, and not lie: though it tarry, wait for it; because it will surely come, it will not tarry.

Habakkuk 2:3

There is no speech nor language, where their voice is not heard.

Their line is gone out through all the earth, and their words to the end of the world. In them hath he set a tabernacle for the sun,

Which is as a bridegroom coming out of his chamber, and rejoiceth as a strong man to run a race.

Psalm 19:3-5

Behold, I will do a new thing; now it shall spring forth; shall ye not know it? I will even make a way in the wilderness, and rivers in the desert.

Isaiah 43:19

The glory of this latter house shall be greater than of the former, saith the LORD of hosts: and in this place will I give peace, saith the LORD of hosts.

Haggai 2:9

I will seek that which was lost, and bring again that which was driven away, and will bind up that which was broken, and will strengthen that which was sick: but I will destroy the fat and the strong; I will feed them with judgment.

Ezekiel 34:16

Behold, the LORD hath proclaimed unto the end of the world, Say ye to the daughter of Zion, Behold, thy salvation cometh; behold, his reward is with him, and his work before him.

And they shall call them, The holy people, The redeemed of the LORD: and thou shalt be called, Sought out, A city not forsaken.

Isaiah 62:11-12

What Are Signs Of The End?

And Jesus answered and said unto them, Take heed that no man deceive you.

For many shall come in my name, saying, I am Christ; and shall deceive many.

And ye shall hear of wars and rumours of wars: see that ye be not troubled: for all these things must come to pass, but the end is not yet.

For nation shall rise against nation, and kingdom against kingdom: and there shall be famines, and pestilences, and earthquakes, in divers places.

All these are the beginning of sorrows.

Then shall they deliver you up to be afflicted, and shall kill you: and ye shall be hated of all nations for my name's sake.

And then shall many be offended, and shall betray one another, and shall hate one another.

And many false prophets shall rise, and shall deceive many.

And because iniquity shall abound, the love of many shall wax cold.

But he that shall endure unto the end, the same shall be saved.

And this gospel of the kingdom shall be preached in all the world for a witness unto all nations; and then shall the end come.

Matthew 24:4-14

Then shall two be in the field; the one shall be taken, and the other left.

Watch therefore: for ye know not what hour your Lord doth come.

Therefore be ye also ready: for in such an hour as ye think not the Son of man cometh.

Matthew 24:40, 42, 44

This know also, that in the last days perilous times shall come.

For men shall be lovers of their own selves, covetous, boasters, proud, blasphemers, disobedient to parents, unthankful, unholy,

Without natural affection, trucebreakers, false accusers, incontinent, fierce, despisers of those that are good.

Traitors, heady, highminded, lovers of pleasures more than lovers of God;

Having a form of Godliness, but denying the power thereof: from such turn away.

II Timothy 3:1-5

Now the Spirit speaketh expressly, that in the latter times some shall depart from the faith, giving heed to seducing spirits, and doctrines of devils;

Speaking lies in hypocrisy; having their conscience seared with a hot iron;

Forbidding to marry, and commanding to abstain from meats, which God hath created to be received with thanksgiving of them which believe and know the truth.

I Timothy 4:1-3

For the time will come when they will not endure sound doctrine; but after their own lusts shall they heap to themselves teachers, having itching ears;

And they shall turn away their ears from the truth, and shall be turned unto fables.

II Timothy 4:3-4

And it shall come to pass in the last days, saith God, I will pour out of my Spirit upon all flesh: and your sons and your daughters shall prophesy, and your young men shall see visions, and your old men shall dream dreams:

And on my servants and on my handmaidens I will pour out in those days of my Spirit; and they shall prophesy:

And I will shew wonders in heaven above, and signs in the earth beneath; blood, and fire, and vapour of smoke:

The sun shall be turned into darkness, and the moon into blood, before that great and notable day of the Lord come:

And it shall come to pass, that whosoever shall call on the name of the Lord shall be saved.

Acts 2:17-21

Behold, the LORD hath proclaimed unto the end of the world, Say ye to the daughter of Zion, Behold, thy salvation cometh; behold, his reward is with him, and his work before him.

And they shall call them, The holy people, The redeemed of the LORD: and thou shalt be called, Sought out, A city not forsaken.

Isaiah 62:11-12

So Christ was once offered to bear the sins of many; and unto them that look for him shall he appear the second time without sin unto salvation.

Hebrews 9:28

The earth shall reel to and fro like a drunkard, and shall be removed like a cottage; and the transgression thereof shall be heavy upon it; and it shall fall, and not rise again.

And it shall come to pass in that day that the LORD shall punish the host of the high ones that are on high, and the kings of the earth upon the earth.

And they shall be gathered together, as prisoners are gathered in the pit, and shall be shut up in the prison, and after many days shall they be visited.

Isaiah 24:20-22

Knowing this first, that there shall come in the last days scoffers, walking after their own lusts,

And saying, Where is the promise of his coming? for since the fathers fell asleep, all things continue as they were from the beginning of the creation.

But, beloved, be not ignorant of this one thing, that one day is with the Lord as a thousand years, and a thousand years as one day.

The Lord is not slack concerning his promise, as some men count slackness; but is longsuffering to us-ward, not willing that any should perish, but that all should come to repentance.

But the day of the Lord will come as a thief in the night; in the which the heavens shall pass away with a great noise, and the elements shall melt with fervent heat, the earth also and the works that are therein shall be burned up.

II Peter 3:3, 4, 8-10

But, beloved, remember ye the words which were spoken before of the apostles of our Lord Jesus Christ;

How that they told you there should be mockers in the last time, who should walk after their own ungodly lusts.

These be they who separate themselves, sensual, having not the Spirit.

But ye, beloved, building up yourselves on your most holy faith, praying in the Holy Ghost,

Keep yourselves in the love of God, looking for the mercy of our Lord Jesus Christ unto eternal life.

Jude 17-21

And likewise also the men, leaving the natural use of the woman, burned in their lust one toward another; men with men working that which is unseemly, and receiving in themselves that recompence of their error which was meet.

Romans 1:27

And in the latter time of their kingdom, when the transgressors are come to the full, a king of fierce countenance, and understanding dark sentences, shall stand up.

Daniel 8:23

And he causeth all, both small and great, rich and poor, free and bond, to receive a mark in their right hand, or in their foreheads: And that no man might buy or sell, save he that had the mark, or the name of the beast, or the number of his name.

Here is wisdom. Let him that hath understanding count the number of the beast: for it is the number of a man; and his number is Six hundred threescore and six.

Revelation 13:16-18

Heaven and earth shall pass away, but my words shall not pass away...

Matthew 24:35

MY PRAYER LIST

MY PRAYER LIST

MY PRAYER LIST

MY PRAYER LIST

MY PRAYER LIST

MY PRAYER LIST

MY PRAYER LIST

MY PRAYER LIST

MY PRAYER LIST

MY PRAYER LIST

MY PRAYER LIST

MY PRAYER LIST

MY PRAYER LIST

MY PRAYER LIST

PERSONAL STUDY NOTES

PERSONAL STUDY NOTES

PERSONAL STUDY NOTES

PERSONAL STUDY NOTES

PERSONAL STUDY NOTES

PERSONAL STUDY NOTES

PERSONAL STUDY NOTES

PERSONAL STUDY NOTES

PERSONAL STUDY NOTES

PERSONAL STUDY NOTES

PERSONAL STUDY NOTES

Other books available from J. Countryman Division,

Word Publishing, Inc.

GOD'S PROMISES for your every need

GOD'S ANSWERS for your life

GOD DOES CARE

PROMESAS DE DIOS
Para Cada Una de Sus Necesidades

RESPUESTAS DE DIOS

GOD'S GIFT for MOTHERS

GOD'S POWER for FATHERS

GOD'S WORD for the FAMILY

GOD'S PROMISES for the GOLDEN YEARS

GOD'S WISDOM for BUSINESS SUCCESS

THANKSGIVING and PRAISE

GOD'S AWESOME PROMISES
for teens and friends

FOREVER IN LOVE